4/3/94

LIBRARIANSHIP:

The Erosion of a Woman's Profession

INFORMATION MANAGEMENT, POLICY, AND SERVICES
Charles R. McClure and Peter Hernon, Editors

Library Performance Accountability and Responsiveness: Essays in Honor of Ernest R. DeProspo
    Charles C. Curran and F. William Summers
Curriculum Initiative: An Agenda and Strategy for Library Media Programs
    Michael B. Eisenberg and Robert E. Berkowitz
Resource Companion to Curriculum Initiative: An Agenda and Strategy for Library
Media Programs
    Michael B. Eisenberg and Robert E. Berkowitz
Information Problem-Solving: The Big Six Skills Approach to Library & Information
Skills Instruction
    Michael B. Eisenberg and Robert E. Berkowitz
The Role and Importance of Managing Information for Competitive Positioning in
Economic Development
    Keith Harman
A Practical Guide to Managing Information for Competitive Positioning in Economic
Development
    Keith Harman
Librarianship: The Erosion of a Woman's Profession
    Roma M. Harris
Microcomputer Software for Performing Statistical Analysis: A Handbook for Supporting
Library Decision Making
    Peter Hernon and John V. Richardson (Editors)
Public Access to Government Information, Second Edition
    Peter Hernon and Charles R. McClure
Statistics: A Component of the Research Process
    Peter Hernon
Statistics for Library Decision Making: A Handbook
    Peter Hernon et al.
Libraries: Partners in Adult Literacy
    Deborah Johnson, Jane Robbins, and Douglas L. Zweizig
The National Research and Education Network (NREN): Research and Policy Perspectives
    Charles R. McClure, Ann P. Bishop, Philip Doty, and Howard Rosenbaum
Library and Information Science Research: Perspectives and Strategies for Improvement
    Charles R. McClure and Peter Hernon (Editors)
U.S. Government Information Policies: Views and Perspectives
    Charles R. McClure, Peter Hernon, and Harold C. Relyea
U.S. Scientific and Technical Information Policies: Views and Perspectives
    Charles R. McClure and Peter Hernon

In preparation
Information Policy: A Framework for Evaluation and Policy Research
    Robert H. Burger
Gatekeepers in Ethnolinguistic Communities
    Cheryl Metayer Duran
Into the Future: The Foundations of Library and Information Services in the Post-
Industrial Era
    Michael Harris and Stanley Hannah
Information Seeking as a Process of Construction
    Carol Kulthau
Records Management and the Library: Issues and Practices
    Candy Schwartz and Peter Hernon
Depository Library Use of Technology: A Practitioner's Perspective
    Jan Swanbeck and Peter Hernon (Editors)
Interpretations of Reference and Bibliographic Work
    Howard White, Marcia Bates, and Patrick Wilson

LIBRARIANSHIP:

The Erosion of a Woman's Profession

Roma M. Harris

School of Library and Information Science
University of Western Ontario
London, Canada

**ABLEX PUBLISHING CORPORATION
NORWOOD, NEW JERSEY**

Library of Congress Cataloging-in-Publication Data

Harris, Roma M.
    Librarianship : the erosion of a woman's profession / Roma M.
Harris.
      p.   cm. -- (Information management, policy, and services)
    Includes bibliographical references and index.
    ISBN 0-89391-840-7 (cl). -- ISBN 0-89391-941-1 (pp)
    1. Women in library science. 2. Sex discrimination against women.
3. Sex discrimination in employment. 4. Library science--Social
aspects. 5. Librarians--Professional ethics. 6. Women in
information science. 7. Women information scientists. 8. Women
librarians.   I. Title. II. Series.
Z682.4.W65H37 1992
0250'.82--dc20   92-15603
                                                                        CIP

Ablex Publishing Corporation
355 Chestnut Street
Norwood, NJ 07648

For Siobhān

Table of Contents

Acknowledgments

This project has occupied my thoughts, on and off, for more than two years and without the support and encouragement I received from friends and colleagues I would have been unable to complete it. There are several people, in particular, to whom I owe a great deal of thanks. Thanks to Gord Nickerson for patiently undertaking online searches for me as I tried to track down the literature on professionalism in several different fields. Thanks to Patricia Dewdney for giving me emotional support and encouragement, even when she was not sure that this project was such a good idea. Thanks to Gillian Michell for reading a draft of this manuscript and offering a number of good suggestions. Thanks to Peter Hernon for encouraging me to write this book and for editing it. Thanks to Jean Tague-Sutcliffe, Dean of the School of Library and Information Science, for creating an environment in which research, including feminist inquiry, is supported and encouraged. And, a special thanks to my mother, Irene Harris, for believing in me, even when she was not sure what I was up to.

Special thanks, too, to King, Riley, Ubu, and Lizzie for standing by me patiently when they would rather have been out for a walk.

Preface

I came to my career as a library science educator through a rather unusual route, having first been educated as a counseling psychologist. Given this background, my research interests, perhaps not surprisingly, led me to investigate the nature of interaction between librarians and their "clients," that is, library patrons. In the process of undertaking this research it became obvious to me that the nature of the service offered in librarianship differs from that seen in other professions in that it is much more centered on the client's need and less focused on the librarian's role as the expert. It was also soon obvious to me that librarians' work and the service they provide are very much undervalued—both by themselves and by others outside this profession.

Through my training in psychology I developed a strong interest in career development theory, particularly as it pertains to the work patterns of women. Given this background, I concluded rather quickly from my observations of librarians' work that the nature of this work and the manner in which it is perceived are very much a function of librarianship's history as a woman's profession. However, whenever I have spoken about the undervaluing of library work being a product of its gendered nature, I am greeted, as often as not, by stony silence. Curiously, there seems to be a great reluctance within this profession to acknowledge the significance of gender in its evolution.

This book, then, is about librarianship, one of the most ignored of the female-intensive professions. At my own peril, perhaps, I have decided to ignore those who will, no doubt, disapprove of a feminist analysis of library work. At present, librarianship is undergoing a profound period of change due, in part, to internally generated pressures as well as to shifts in the economy and the impact of technology. It seems to me that the processes shaping the future of this field cannot be fully understood by ignoring the fact that for more than 100 years library work in North America has been women's work.

During the first half of this century, librarianship, along with nursing, teaching, and social work, offered educated women a means by which they could legitimately enter the paid labor force. However, as career opportunities for women have become increasingly diverse in recent years, the female-intensive professions have become less attractive, especially in comparison with more glamorous male professions, such as law and medicine, which offer their members considerably more status and much greater earning power. There is, in fact, considerable evidence that women's fields, such as nursing, are losing their competitive edge in attracting new recruits. And, even though we have entered what has been widely touted as the "information age," there is little evidence to suggest that librarianship is thriving, at present, in North America. Indeed, the number of library workers has actually decreased in the United States since the mid-1980s.

Failing to acknowledge this decline, some members of the library community have tried to put a brave face on things by describing the developments taking place in the field as signs of progress and greater professionalism. There are few, however, who give voice to another interpretation of these events; that is, that the increasing marginalization of librarianship is due to the fact that it is a woman's profession. What has been ignored, by and large, by the members of this occupation is that women's work, including their own, is not highly valued in this culture. Indeed, because women's endeavor is accorded so little weight in what remains very much a male world, the ability of librarians to exercise control in the information sector of the economy or to influence the development of information policy is extremely limited.

Although painful, it seems to me to be worth the trouble to examine the field's development from this perspective for without a thoughtful look at the rapid changes the profession is undergoing, librarianship, at least as we now know it, may be irrevocably lost. By failing to acknowledge the significance of its identity as a female profession, librarians may soon discover not only that they are no longer in control of those aspects of information work once uniquely their own, but that they must stand by helplessly while the avenues to information they once made available to a wide community of users slowly wither away.

Roma Harris
March 1991

PART I

Pressing for Change from Within: The Professionalization Movement

Much of the internal pressure for change in librarianship has come from librarians' desire to achieve professional status for their occupation. Like nursing and social work, librarianship is characterized by a pervasive anxiety about its image and identity. As a result, librarians often urge one another to undertake such tasks as monitoring the popular media for portrayals of unflattering occupational stereotypes. The literature is also full of examples of librarians exhorting their colleagues to adopt a "more professional" manner. However, by far the most significant source of change within this occupation stems from the attempts of its members to mimic the higher status male professions.

By adopting many of the characteristics of occupations such as law and medicine, librarians are reshaping their own field. Their efforts to "professionalize" librarianship have resulted, for example, in such an emphasis on the scientific basis of librarianship that even the very name of the occupation is being altered. Professionalization has also produced a system of differential rewards in the field. Those aspects of library work that are considered to be the most "masculine," that is, those involving technology and management, are also the most highly valued, while the more "feminine" tasks such as children's services and cataloging are not held in such high regard. In effect, then, the professionalization movement in librarianship represents an attempt to escape its female identity.

In Part I discussion centers on the impact of the professionalization movement in librarianship and the attempt to control the public image of this and other female-intensive fields. The meaning of professionalism and its ramifications for librarianship are discussed in Chapter 1, as is the lack of acknowledgment of the field's female identity in both the scholarly and professional literature. In Chapter 2, the nature and value accorded to the work undertaken in the female-intensive fields is described, along with a discussion of the various methods of status climbing that have been embraced in these occupations. The efforts to control the gateways to entry into the female-intensive professions through education and licensing are examined in Chapter 3. In Chapter 4 there is a discussion of the self-doubt and self-blame which characterize the female-intensive professions. The attempts to manage the occupational image of these fields is described in Chapter 5 and in Chapter 6 there is an analysis of the success of the library unions and associations in achieving the goals of their members.

In Part II (Chapters 7 to 9) the focus shifts away from these internal pressures for change and onto two important developments which are having a profound impact on the future of librarianship: the rapid advance of computing technology and the resulting commodification of information.

CHAPTER 1

In Pursuit of Status

Librarians, like nurses and social workers, have for many years been pre-occupied with questions of image and status. Arising from this preoccupation is the particularly nagging question of whether or not these occupations constitute "true" professions. As will be evident later in this chapter, the answer to this question has been elusive. Indeed, before an answer can even be attempted it is necessary to consider just what is meant by the term "profession" and how its various definitions have been applied to librarianship and the other female-intensive fields.

The expression, "female-intensive," will be used throughout this book to refer to occupations in which a very high proportion of the workers are women. There are a number of such occupations within the clerical, sales, and service sectors of the labor force and they are described as female-intensive to indicate that although they are numerically dominated by women, they are controlled, to a large extent, by men. The male control in these fields is evident in two respects. First of all, the total number of men who are employed as librarians, nurses, public school teachers, or telephone operators, for example, is relatively small, yet they tend to hold a disproportionately large number of the positions of authority in these ocupations. Second, and perhaps more importantly, powerful male-dominated professions, such as law and medicine, tend to exercise considerable influence over the organization of the women's fields and the activities that are undertaken within them.

Among all the female-intensive occupations, those in which there seems to be the greatest concern over questions of image and prestige (or the lack of it) are in the group sometimes referred to as the "semi" or "near profes-sions." In fact, the literatures of librarianship, social work, and nursing, as well as those of home economics and public school teaching, are replete with examples of what might best be described as an obsession with status.

The extent of this obsession is evident not only in the relentless production of articles about whether or not these occupations are real professions, but also in the various "how-to" publications that describe methods by which the members of these occupations can enhance their image.

THE PURSUIT OF PROFESSIONALISM

Some critics, irritated by this preoccupation with status, have urged their colleagues to abandon the issue of professionalism in favor of more meaningful pursuits. Stokes (1967), for example, reminded his fellow librarians that "status has only to be sought when it is not freely given. To demand it is usually not so much the sign of an inferiority complex as a demonstration of inferiority" (p. 3600). Moreover, he suggested that because

> librarianship is essentially a practical profession...it has as much need for good craftsmanship and as little need for high-flown theory as has the job of digging a hole in the road. I am not greatly concerned that we should struggle to establish the idea of a profession as opposed to a trade or craft. (Ibid.)

In a similar vein, Vagianos (1973) chided librarians with his observation that "the insecurity and self-consciousness associated with our never-ending identity crisis is misguided, a problem of our own making" (p. 391).

Despite such reprimands, the discussion of image and status has continued unabated in the female-intensive fields. Librarians, for instance, "have been absorbed to a marked degree, from 1876 to the present, with the question of professionalization" (Garrison, 1979, p. 186), in spite of the fact that in 1876 Melvil Dewey himself announced that "the time has at last come when a librarian may, without assumption, speak of *his* occupation as a profession" (p. 5; emphasis mine). Nurses, too, according to Hughes, Hughes, and Deutscher (1958) have, for many years, continued their "fruitless argument" over whether or not nursing is a profession (p. 4). All of this stems, of course, from a basic insecurity among the members of these occupations for, as Katz (1969) pointed out, "few professionals talk as much about being professionals as those whose professional stature is in doubt" (p. 71).

WHAT CONSTITUTES A PROFESSION?

At the root of the seemingly endless propensity for self-examination in the women's fields lies the commonly held, but seldom expressed, view that female occupations are somehow "less" than other, usually male, types of work. In particular, there is a widespread perception that librarians, nurses, and social workers are not really professionals. This raises the question, of course, as to what constitutes a profession. While this begs an answer, a clear response has not been forthcoming because the criteria that are normally used to judge professionalism vary so considerably. Hence, there is as yet no resolution to this debate. For example, in assessing the professional status of librarianship not only did Gwinnup (1974) conclude that it is not a true profession, but Flanagan (1973) suggested that rather than considering themselves to be professionals, librarians should think of themselves instead as merely "advanced technicians." On the other hand, a number of people have argued that librarians are de facto professionals because their field is organized as a profession and possesses many of the attributes of occupations such as medicine and law (see, for example, Vice, 1988; Birdsall, 1980; Wilson, 1984).

THEORIES OF PROFESSIONALISM

Much of the difficulty in deciding whether or not an occupation has attained the status of a profession arises from the use of outmoded sociological theories of work, especially the so-called "trait" theory of professionalism. According to this view, professions can be distinguished from other occupations through the application of a set of criteria. Although these criteria which are used to distinguish professions from nonprofessions may vary, lists of the relevant traits normally include the following: an advanced university-based education, a unique body of abstract knowledge, a code of ethics for practitioners, an orientation toward service, autonomy in the practice of work, and an association of members through which control is exercised over who is authorized to practice and how such practice is to be conducted. Within some versions of trait theory, according to Winter (1988), it is also assumed that "there is a state of being—a rather exalted one—called 'full professionalization,' and that the most traditional and longest established professional groups have attained this state" (p. 21). In other words, occupations which exhibit such characteristics as a specialized education within a university setting or a code of ethics may be judged to be outright professions or at least to be more professional than occupations in which these characteristics are not evident.

When the trait theorists have turned their attention to the fields in which women are employed in significantly higher numbers than men, they have generally found these occupations to be lacking some or all of the professional attributes. Nursing, social work, public school teaching, and librarianship have been repeatedly found to fall short in comparison with what Goode (1969) called the "four great *person* professions: law, medicine, the ministry and university teaching" (p. 267).[1] As a result, the term "semi-profession" is sometimes used when referring to occupations, such as librarianship, by which it is implied that although they are to be distinguished·from less cerebral fields of work, they do not measure up to the true professions.

Goode (1969) argued that the "two central generating qualities" of professionalism are "a basic body of abstract knowledge" and the "ideal of service" (p. 277). Underlying this view is one of the most significant assumptions of trait theory which is that occupations that are excluded from the professional elite for failing to exhibit the requisite attributes can move toward greater professionalization by adopting these characteristics. In other words, occupations whose members devote themselves to the acquisition of these traits may be transformed into professions. As a result of this assumption many occupational groups, including nurses, librarians, and social workers, have dedicated much of their collective energies over the past 50 or 60 years to the pursuit of such attributes. In spite of their efforts, however, they may never achieve "full" professionalization. Goode claimed, for instance, that librarianship would always fall short of true professionalism because

> although individual librarians have been learned, and librarians in general are as dedicated to knowledge as they are committed to service, the public is not convinced that there is a basic science of librarianship: the skill is thought to be only clerical or administrative. (p. 286)[2]

It appears then that even though librarianship and the other female-intensive fields may actually possess the characteristics deemed by Goode and other trait theorists to be those of a professional occupation, they may continue to be excluded from the professional ranks simply by virtue of the way they are commonly perceived.

Problems with Trait Theory

The arguments as to whether or not the female-intensive fields possess the attributes of professions, and to what degree, have been the preoccupa-

---

[1] Glazer (1974) reduced this list even further, distinguishing law and medicine, the "major" professions, from all other "minor" professions.

[2] Goode (1969) was even more damning of public school teaching and commented that "the school teacher (especially in the primary schools) has a similar relationship to her knowledge base, which is not so much the curriculum content. . . but the technique and principles of pedagogy. This content is, however, relatively small in amount and shallow intellectually" (p. 286).

tion of many analysts in these occupations over the last three decades in spite of the fact that for a number of years the trait approach to the study of occupations has been subjected to some harsh criticism. The problems with trait theory can be summed up best by Freidson's observation that not only do most definitions of professionalism "overlap in the elements, traits or attributes they include" but that tallies of these traits show "a persistent lack of consensus about which traits are to be emphasised" (Freidson, 1983, p. 21).

Despite its shortcomings trait theory remains a common source of self-inflicted anxiety in all the female-intensive occupations. In the literature of librarianship, for example, "the trait approach is dominant," it "per-sists, almost untouched by reflective criticism" and "is ubiquitous" (Winter, 1988, p. 39). In social work, and nursing too, there continues to be a very heavy reliance on trait theory which forms the basis for most discussions of professionalism. In fact, Miller (1988, p. 18) recently outlined "a model for professionalism for nursing" in which she listed the characteristics necessary for the professionalization of nursing, nearly all of which have been used for years by trait theorists to justify the exclusion of this occupation from the elite category of the professions.

The ongoing use of trait theory reflects an obvious discomfort within the female professions over their status vis-à-vis the high prestige fields. Indeed, some of the popularity of trait theory may stem from the fact that it suggests a route for achieving occupational greatness. In other words, by acquiring certain characteristics these lesser occupations also might share in the glory currently reserved for physicians and lawyers. Judging by the volume of library and nursing literature published on this theme, there are many nurses and librarians who believe in this approach to occupational development. Winter (1988), however, recognized this seductive aspect of trait theory and warned that when models of professionalization are accepted "naively as scorecards to rate occupations, they fail to lead beyond the most obvious sorting devices; and this is not sociology, but rather a form of status seeking" (p. 140).

Alternatives to Trait Theory

One of the major difficulties with the trait theory is that it treats "profession" as though it were "a generic concept rather than a changing historic concept" (Freidson, 1983, p. 22). An alternative way of thinking is to recognize that "a profession isn't a kind of occupation but a complex set of procedures for controlling an occupation" (Winter, 1988, p. 44). As Esta-brook (1989) pointed out, occupations that are seen to be professions "achieve that recognition as a result of ongoing struggles to achieve control over their work, to control the external markets in which their services are delivered, and to achieve social and political status" (p. 287). In fact, it is precisely as a result of this struggle for control that some fields claim to be more professional than others or emphasize particular attributes as being more significant determinants of professionalism than others. When viewed within this context then it is not surprising that

> rather different concepts of profession would be advanced by occupations seeking the rewards of a professional label than by other occupations attempting to preserve the rewards they have already won. (Freidson, 1983, p. 28)

This perspective enables one to examine how different occupations use the patina of professionalism and select various "professional" traits to protect their interests by exerting control over others or to win greater rewards for their members. Consider, for example, the ongoing battle for control being fought between physicians and nurses. Physicians, members of a powerful, long-standing profession, argue that their knowledge base encompasses that of nurses and that they have the right, therefore, to control what goes on in all medical practice. In other words, by virtue of their knowledge base they feel justified in controlling not only their own work but also that of nurses and other medical practitioners, such as physiotherapists. Nurses, on the other hand, who are members of an aspiring or "would-be" profession, claim that their role in promoting general health and well-being in their clients makes their field distinct from that practiced by physicians. As such, they believe that they are entitled not only to control their own occupation but to work as autonomous "professionals," independent of physicians. Thus, as Freidson's analysis suggests, physicians emphasize the similarity of their knowledge base with that of nursing in order to protect their interests, while nurses emphasize the differences between their occupations in order to attain greater autonomy.

OCCUPATIONAL AUTHORITY

As the nursing example suggests, in order to understand the development of an occupation it is far more revealing to study how it is controlled (both from within as well as by the external environment which impinges on it) than to merely examine the degree to which it possesses the various attributes of professionalism. This is particularly true for the female-intensive occupations since the primary feature that distinguishes them from the more powerful male professions is not so much the degree to which they possess particular traits but rather how they are controlled. Indeed, the women's professions have all faced challenges from outside groups that have attempted to exert control over their activities. In spite of these pressures, however, each of these fields has been able to exercise a considerable degree of authority within its own domain.

According to Winter (1988), there are two types of occupational author-ity: normative authority in which members of a group "share ways of thinking, problem solving, and types of professional behavior" (p. 58), and structural authority which is the "legal power with which the occu-pation has been vested by legislative bodies and government agencies" (p. 59). Although nursing, social work, and librarianship all possess norma-tive authority (just as is the case in medicine and law), they have some-what less structural authority. In other words, the legal control of these occupations through procedures, such as licensing, is not as firmly en-trenched as it is in the more established male professions.

Winter noted that when occupations, such as librarianship, are seen to have fallen short of having achieved full professional status, it is usually because they have been judged almost solely on the basis of structural authority. However, just because some of the female-intensive fields have not been able to exercise the level of legal control found in the male pro-fessions does not mean that they possess no other control mechanisms through which they can monitor and, to some extent, police the activities of their members. For instance, the gateways into each of these occupa-tions are controlled to a considerable degree through the educational process (the nature of which is discussed in detail in Chapter 3).

FLAWED ANALYSES OF THE FEMALE FIELDS

It seems then that when carefully examined, many of the judgments that have been made about professionalism in the female-intensive fields have been flawed. Trait theorists have simply failed, historically, to acknowl-edge that social work, nursing, and librarianship do indeed exhibit many of the characteristics that are used to distinguish professions from other occupations. In many respects these occupations are not all that different from the elite, male-dominated professions to which they are so often compared, except insofar as they are valued. To use just one example: Consider the criterion of research, the building block of an occupation's knowledge base. Nursing, librarianship, and social work have all been subjected to serious criticism about their research literatures; criticism which, at least in the case of librarianship, is open to challenge. For in-stance, Winter (1988) argued that

> the alleged fact that practitioners do not contribute to research literatures cannot be held against any occupation, for it is normally teachers and scholars who carry out this function and not practitioners. Practitioner literature is normally characterized by a mix of policy and case reporting, and this is true not only of librarianship but of law and medicine as well. Thus empirical findings showing that practitioners do not contribute significantly to research

> literature cannot be used as evidence against a claim for professional status. (p. 101)

Furthermore,

> in comparison with other occupations, working librarians make substantial contributions to the research literature. (p. 102)

Thus,

> we see the outlines of a body of literature that is not very different from the research literatures of many other fields... The only way librarianship seems to differ substantially is in relying more, not less, on the practitioner. (p. 106)

The upshot of Winter's analysis is that the criterion of research has been applied somewhat arbitrarily to exclude librarianship from the professions, raising a question as to whether similarly biased judgments have been made about the lack of professional characteristics in the other female-intensive fields.

THE VALUE OF WOMEN'S WORK

If it is true that the women's professions have received somewhat less than evenhanded treatment from trait theorists, what accounts for this apparent bias? In the case of nursing, one obvious explanation is that the struggle for occupational control and nursing's lack of status within the health care infrastructure is largely a function of its female identity rather than because of its failure to acquire professional characteristics. This connection was made rather explicitly by Brown (1975), who observed that

> the health service industry is run by a small minority. It is run primarily by physicians, who have traditionally held the power, but also by the increasingly powerful hospital administrators, insurance company directors, government regulators, medical school educators and corporation managers. Most of these people are men. (p. 173)

Nerad (1988) pointed to a similar scenario in home economics, another female-intensive occupation. She noted that the rise and fall in the fortunes of a home economics department within a large American university was due largely to the factor of gender in the ranking of academic departments. In fact, it is generally true that in male-run institutions, such as universities, male departments, whether academic (e.g., economics), professional (e.g., engineering) or support services (e.g., computing centers), fare better in the allocation of resources than do female departments (e.g., nursing) or support services (e.g., the library).

As is suggested by these examples, if one is to make sense of the status accorded to the female-intensive occupations, it is essential to consider their membership base. As a result, even though the control theory of occupational development is useful in explaining the pressures that are faced by a great many fields, it is not particularly helpful in accounting for the special circumstances of the female-intensive occupations except insofar as it alerts one to the attempts by other, usually male, fields to exercise control over them. In other words, to forget that occupations, such as librarianship, home economics, and nursing, are special because they are primarily populated by women is a serious omission in any attempt to understand their development.

LABOR FORCE SEGREGATION

The male professions, of course, are not immune to external pressures or to anxieties over status and image on the part of their members. Even in engineering, one of the most heavily male-populated professions, dire predictions about the future can be found in the literature of the field. Zwiep 1980), for example, warned that unless engineers are successful in defending their professionalism

> they will soon become the handmaidens of any number of outside alien inter-
> ests and pressures. Furthermore, their independence and integrity will be
> undermined and their authority diminished. (p. 29)

Others, such as Krislov (1981), lament the lack of definition and low status associated with the title of "engineer," while Lidgate (1988) complained about the low salaries in the profession. Such concerns are relative, however, particularly in light of the fact that not only do engineers enjoy a considerably higher status than most other occupational groups, but they are compensated at a higher rate than most others as well. To cite just one example, in comparison with faculty members in *all* other disciplines, those who pursue an academic career in engineering in the United States receive salaries that have "topped the pay scales" for six years in a row (Blum, 1989).

Not only are members of the female-intensive fields poorly paid relative to male-dominated professions, such as engineering, law, and medicine, but within the women's professions the most prestigious and highly paid positions are generally held by men. This pattern of intraoccupational segregation was explained 30 years ago by Rossi (1961) who observed that women depress the status of an occupation because theirs is a depressed status in the society as a whole, and those occupations in which women are found in large numbers are not seen as seriously competing with other professions for personnel and resources. It is for this reason that professions such as education, social work, and librarianship develop within themselves a division of labor and accompanying status along sex lines. (p. 381)

Noting the presence of male enclaves within the library world, Hildenbrand (1985) observed that, historically, men have been

disproportionately represented in academic librarianship and underrepresented in work with children in either public or school library settings. Those areas with the highest proportion of men were, of course, seen as the most prestigious, and the most professional. (p. 191)

Similar divisions have been evident in social work, too, due in part to an influx of men into the field which was deliberately encouraged during the early 1970s. The result of this, according to Fortune and Hanks (1988), was to raise the field's overall prestige and salary levels,

but men were the primary beneficiaries, with little benefit to women. . . male clinicians were found to move into nonclinical positions more often than women and, regardless of position, soon earned more than women. (p. 221)

KEEPING SILENT ABOUT WOMEN

As we approach the 21st century, Rossi's comments about women's impact on their places of work are still relevant. Intraoccupational segregation by gender is still very much in evidence throughout the labor force, and the field of librarianship offers no exception to this rule. Today, not only is it still possible to identify differences in the male and female specialties within the field (see, for example, Hildenbrand, 1989a), but the female specialties, as well as the types of libraries in which greater numbers of women are found, continue to be less prestigious than the male areas of specialization (Harris, Monk, and Austin, 1986).

In spite of the prevalence of these patterns, however, and the very strong association between women's work and low rates of compensation, the impact of women's presence in the female-intensive fields is usually ignored. Even in the sociology of work,

the historical relationship of professionalization and patriarchy remains largely implicit in most feminist studies, and largely ignored outside feminism. (Hearn, 1982, p. 186)

And, in the literatures of the female-intensive occupations, their female-ness is seldom mentioned "as if in some modern version of Victorian manners" (Bennett, 1988, p. 80). One finds, for example, that when librarians debate with one another about the best strategies to enhance their status or to gain professional recognition,

> the dominant influence of women on librarianship has been strangely shunted aside, buried under a multitude of words concerning recruitment, accreditation, library school curriculums, and other factors thought to be inhibiting professionalization. (Hildenbrand, 1985, p. 186)

Hildenbrand's explanation for this is that if women's presence were to be acknowledged it might have a "negative impact on professional status" (p. 195). In fact, she noted that despite the large number of women who have worked in the profession,

> library history emphasizes either leadership or fields such as academic librarianship, both of which are disproportionately male. The few female leaders have generally been ignored even in the standard reference sources. (p. 195)

What Hildenbrand has suggested, basically, is that to draw attention to the female composition of a field is to discredit it. In other words, focusing on the presence of women in female-intensive occupations represents a threat to the already shaky status of these occupations. Alternatively, the lack of interest in women within the women's professions may simply reflect the general lack of status accorded to women in society as a whole, thereby making them a subject unworthy of detailed study by any group other than feminists who are, by definition, interested in women's activities.

Whatever the reason for it, the tendency to ignore the issue of gender in studies of occupational development is a disturbing one. One example of such a study is Wilson's (1982) often-cited analysis of the stereotypes and status of U.S. librarians. Although she acknowledged that women comprise the majority of librarians, and that women and men tend to be segregated in the workplace, with women found more often in small libraries with small budgets, Wilson suggested that this segregation is largely a matter of choice "for the sake of convenience" on the part of female librarians. With this as her rationale she then sidestepped the whole issue of gender and occupational status with the following disclaimer:

> Because the library profession does not have the power to change this situation of choice for convenience reasons, it will not be discussed further. The focus of this book is on factors that can be changed. (p. 131)

Surely one would expect that a study of status and stereotypes would include gender as a primary focus of discussion when the focus of the investigation is an occupation which has been predominantly populated by women and subjected to harsh stereotypes as a result. As one reviewer put it, "what Wilson's analysis has failed to consider is *why* our society regards librarians as unimportant" (Blake, 1983, p. 1345). In Wilson's defense, however, the bypassing of the issue of gender is not at all unusual in her field, nor is it atypical of nursing and social work.

THE FEMINIZATION HYPOTHESIS

One exception to the general pattern of ignoring the impact of women in the development of the female-intensive fields is the feminization hypothesis. According to this view, when large numbers of women are employed in an occupation, they leave their stamp on the types of work done and how the occupation is organized. For example, in her analysis of the development of public libraries in North America, Garrison (1979) argued that the "female dominance of librarianship did much to shape the inferior and precarious status of the public library as a culture resource; it evolved into a marginal kind of public amusement service" (p. 174). She claimed that

> although librarianship certainly has shown a number of professional traits, significant elements of a truly professional code of service still are missing. Specifically lacking are a professional sense of commitment to work, a drive to lead rather than to serve, and a clear-cut conception of professional rights and responsibilities. The feminization of library work is a major cause of the deficiencies. (p. 188)[3]

During the latter part of the last century, women were recruited into teaching, nursing, social work, and librarianship because they comprised a relatively large pool of cheap, educated labor. In order to justify their recruitment, Garrison argued, "femininity was newly defined on a vocational basis" (p. 184), which means, in other words, that a "facilitating ideology" was developed. Within this ideological framework the myth was maintained that the "feminine mind and nature were innately suited" to particular kinds of work.

> Thus it was decided that teaching was just like mothering. . . women doctors and nurses were intuitively kind, sympathetic, and delicate of touch. Women social workers expressed inborn feminine qualities of love, charity and idealism. Factory, business, and clerical work fit the feminine nature, for women

---

[3] Clearly, Garrison's version of the feminization hypothesis relies very heavily on trait theory in order to account for the shortcomings of librarianship.

were naturally industrious, sober, and nimble-fingered, as well as better able than men to endure the boredom of detailed or repetitive tasks. (Garrison, 1979, p. 177)

The legacy of these claims is a set of occupational stereotypes that are sufficiently powerful to keep women in and men out of the women's professions.

Essentially, the feminization hypothesis blames the women in the women's fields for the lack of professional status attained by their occupations. As Schiller (1974) put it, "the predominance of women appears as the *cause*, rather than as the *result* of the profession's marginality" (p. 124). This is illustrated, for example, in Castledine's (1989) comment on the nursing profession in which he observed that "the outcome of th[e] female domination of nursing has in many ways suppressed its development" (p. 16).

The feminization hypothesis is derived largely from personality theory, on the basis of which it can be argued that the developments in the female-intensive fields have taken place because of the characteristics women exhibit due to their socialization experiences. It is assumed, then, that because women are brought up to behave in ways that may inhibit their ambitions and encourage self-sacrifice, the fields in which they work in any significant numbers will come to reflect such "womanly" patterns of behavior and thereby be limited in development. While such notions may appear to be somewhat outmoded today, arguments of this sort are still very much in evidence in the literatures of the female professions. In the field of nursing, for instance, it has been suggested that nurses suffer from "our feminine socialization which makes us passive, less able to deal incisively with the male-dominated society, health care system, and patient care norms" (Partridge, 1978, p. 356). Putting it even more bluntly, Castledine (1989) argued that in nursing the "preferred female personality traits are the opposite of those required for professional achievement" (p. 16). Comparable observations are also found in other women's fields. For instance, in a school library journal it was suggested that women adapt their behavior and values "in deference to male authority" (Silver, 1988, p. 21) thereby inhibiting their own vocational development as well as the development of the fields in which they work.

THE DEVALUATION OF WOMEN

The primary advantage of the feminization hypothesis is that it recognizes that the unique characteristic of the female-intensive occupations is that they are, in fact, female. The hypothesis is seriously flawed, however, in that it fails to take into account the ways in which women's work is valued in this society; a factor that is a much more important determinant of the low status of occupations, such as librarianship and social work, than whether or not they exhibit the characteristics of the higher status male professions.

The devaluation of women and their contributions to the workplace is at the root of the feminization hypothesis and is very much in evidence in Garrison's analysis of public librarians. According to Garrison (1979),

> the feminization of public librarianship did much to shape and stunt the development of an important American cultural institution. Because the first generations of library women did not question their sex-typed roles, the socially designated femininity that library women elected to act out had a major influence upon the formation of the public library's 'homey' atmosphere, its patrons, its book collection, and its 'helpful' staff. (p. 241)

However, despite her general condemnation of the women who influenced the development of public libraries, Garrison did recognize that at least some of the difficulties which faced these early librarians was the result of the value attached to their work. She noted, for instance, that

> it is absurd to think that a society which invariably barred women from equality in law, religion, politics, or the economic structure, which denied them even the right to vote, would accord power or prestige to women's work or to women's vocational spheres in the community. (p. 184)

MIMICKING THE MALE PROFESSIONS

Because relatively little value is attached to women's endeavor, it is no coincidence that efforts to enhance the status of the female-intensive fields tend, for the most part, to involve strategies that mimic developments in higher status fields, particularly those in the male professions. In fact, one might describe many of the developments in the women's occupations as attempts to abandon their female identity in favor of a rather more masculine "professional" identity.

In librarianship, Allen (1984) noted that while

> there is much merit and sense in the view that librarians should be content to be, and strive to be accepted as librarians, it would seem to be inevitable that the establishment and maintenance of claims for equivalence in salaries and conditions of service with other professional groups must rely substantially on the ability of librarians to demonstrate their worth by criteria intelligible to, and commonly used by, such other groups. . . . Qualifications, research, involvement in institutional activities outside the library, and publications, must inevitably be accepted by librarians as proper obligations if they aspire to professional or academic status. (p. 9)

Similarly, Garrison's (1979) solution to the status and salary problems facing public librarianship was to

> modify the conventional role of the public librarian...(and)...to establish librarianship on a scientifically oriented, abstract-knowledge base and to train the librarian as the indispensable expert in knowledge retrieval. (p. 241)

Allen and Garrison's suggestions illustrate a common theme in the literatures of the female-intensive fields: The need to adopt the values and definitions of the higher prestige male professions in order to advance their own status.

The blind pursuit of professionalism may not necessarily lead aspiring occupations to the exalted state suggested by trait theory. Simply adopting the characteristics of the "true" professions, such as law and medicine, does not ensure that an occupation like nursing or social work will attain either the status or financial rewards enjoyed by these other professions. As Shera (1976) reminded librarians,

> we have ransacked the literature of professionalism and written seemingly endless pages to prove or to disprove that librarianshp is or is not qualified to rank with medicine, law, and theology...What we have failed to observe is that the term profession itself is suffering a dual fate. It has lost much of its glamor because almost every human activity, in an effort to achieve prestige, calls itself a profession. (p. 282)

In fact, the failure of the professionalism strategy to lead to greater status and financial reward is illustrated by the case of psychiatric social work, the development of which was explicitly modeled after other professional fields in the hope that by adopting their characteristics it would come to be accorded a similar status. Although it was developed so as to include various structural controls, the founders of psychiatric social work

> soon realized that female social workers would not achieve the autonomy, the power, or the prestige that the psychiatrists they worked with would claim for themselves. (Glazer and Slater, 1987, p. 167)

ABANDONING THE CORE OF THE FEMALE FIELDS

It is clear that the status of the female-intensive fields cannot be understood simply by using the attribute test for the professions. Such a test is flawed not only because of the difficulties inherent in trait theory itself, but also because the presence of the so-called "professional" traits in the female fields has not resulted in any value being added to the work undertaken in these occupations. In fact, many analysts of the female-intensive occupations are critical of the pursuit of professionalism because there is an increasing recognition that through such an exercise the primary goals of these occupations may be lost.

For instance, social workers are increasingly entering private practice in order to attain a greater level of autonomy in the conduct of their work than is possible within the bureaucratic structures of most hospitals and social service agencies. This pursuit of autonomy is very much in keeping with the trait model of professionalism. However, it represents a threat to the service ethic that is at the foundation of social work. Although he was not critical of professionalism per se, Blumenstein (1988) observed that with the loss of experienced social workers to private practice, the social work profession is less and less able to provide services to its traditional client base, that is, to people who are economically marginal. In other words, by selling their professional wares privately, social workers are excluding those who may be most in need because they are unable to pay the fees for such services.

Similar concerns have been raised about the trend away from the traditionally "free" services provided by librarians toward either fee-based services in libraries, or even more dramatically, the marketing of information as a commodity in the private sector. Thus, as will be discussed at length in Chapter 8, rather than making information available to anyone who wishes to have it, librarians and others in the information economy are beginning to segment the consumer market into those who can pay and those who cannot.

The other manifestation of professionalism that has resulted in a move away from direct service in the female-intensive occupations is the result of the desire on the part of many people in these fields to achieve greater status and remuneration through advancement up the managerial ladder. As Winter (1988) pointed out,

> one of the more general patterns in most professional work finds the more advanced worker having more colleague than client contact. Indeed higher status work may be almost totally removed from clients; this is true in librarianship, at least where administration is the only path to advancement. (p. 83)

A similar pattern has been observed in nursing where shifting the focus onto administration and/or research and away from direct service to patients is seen as a means for nurses to "demonstrate their equality with the world outside nursing" with the result that "nursing care has been neglected and separated" (Castledine, 1989, p. 16). According to Partridge (1978), the field of nursing has given over patient-related practice to paraprofessionals. Seeing this as abandoning women's values (as well as traditional nursing values) in favor of a male definition of professionalism, she noted that based on a misdiagnosis of what would give us power and status as professionals, we have set about taking on all the attributes of our male and 'fully professional' colleagues in the traditional professions. (p. 357)

The Ideal of Service

What these patterns suggest, paradoxically, is that professionalism may almost inevitably lead to a movement away from service which, for many people, represents the core of the female-intensive professions. As noted earlier, one of the two central characteristics of professions proposed by Goode (1969) is the ideal of service. Curiously, however, this ideal, usually considered to be the most prominent attribute of women's work, was thought by Goode to be missing in the female-intensive fields. He argued, in fact, that these occupations lack "the dedication to service the society considers necessary for a profession" (p. 267). And, in a somewhat confusing reversal of Goode's argument, Garrison (1979) concluded that public librarianship fails the attribute test for professionalism because its members favor service over "a drive to lead" (p. 188). It seems then, that among trait theorists, what constitutes "professional service" is unclear.

The situation becomes somewhat less confusing, however, when one looks closely at Goode's notion of service. Within his analytic framework, service is not a matter of an exchange of information or assistance between two equal partners. Rather, it conforms to the "expert" or paternalistic model of professionalism in which the professional knows what is best for the client. Critics of this view suggest that such a perspective on service "is intended to establish the dominance of the professional over the layman, to maintain the mystery of the profession and to keep the layman in ignorance" (Nelson, 1980, p. 2032). The manner of practice in the female-intensive professions offers an alternative to this elitist vision. Here one is more likely to encounter a sort of "democratic professionalism" in which practitioners do not "dictate what clients must do, but discover what the clients need and fulfil these needs by using specialized knowledge and skills" (Hanks and Schmidt, 1975, p. 186). Thus, librarians, for example, "provide access to information and generally leave it to the client to analyze and use this information effectively" (McDermott, 1984, p. 20).

One important difference, then, between the female-intensive professions and the traditionally male professions lies in the degree of control exercised over the helping process. The female fields have been stigmatized for being helpful and "non-assertive in nature, rather than authoritative in . . . provision of service" (Ibid.). Unfortunately, the nonpaternalistic type of service orientation which has traditionally characterized not only librarianship, but also nursing and social work, is presently under siege by those who wish to advance these fields by embracing the model of professionalism exemplified by lawyers and physicians. Since the alternative, that is, the male model of professionalism, involves "establishing a monopoly over the service it provides" (Ibid.), it would seem that those in the female-intensive fields who advocate such a position may, in the long run, harm the users of their services. This harm would be comparable to that inflicted by lawyers and physicians who are often unable to respond adequately to their clients' needs because they cannot construe these needs from the clients' perspective but only from that of their own profession.

CONCLUSION

The question all of this raises for librarians, social workers, and nurses is "will the price for greater status be paid by clients?" In other words, if the female-intensive occupations adopt the male model of professionalism, must they inevitably abandon their democratic service tradition?

Critics of professionalism argue that whether or not fields, such as nursing or librarianship, are professions is a "non-issue." Because librarians, for instance, have chosen for many years to organize their work as a profession, Wilson (1984) argued that this is what is important,

> not whether it meets every characteristic associated with professions to the highest degree. No profession achieves that level of fidelity to the professional model. What counts is that librarianship is organized as a profession and *uses the methods* of a profession to achieve its occupational goals. (p. 563)

Thus, for Wilson the term "profession" simply means "a way of organizing work in order to accomplish occupational goals" (p. 563). Nelson (1980), too, was critical of professionalism, referring to it as "a false goal" (p. 2033). In fact, she suggested that

> trying to meet the attributes of a profession as laid down by sociologists is a waste of time and energy...the real question is not whether librarianship is a 'profession,' but rather do we as librarians value our work, do we believe it can be done even better than at present, and do we want to improve it? (p. 2033)

Similar arguments have been expressed by social workers and nurses, nearly all of whom agree that by emphasizing professionalism as the way to achieve greater prestige, the essence or value of the service-oriented women's fields may be damaged. About social work, for instance, Lause (1979) observed that the field's "ability to contribute to the development of a more just and humanistic society is currently inhibited by a...preoccupation with status enhancement" (p. 546). In fact, Lause's remark could have been aimed equally as well at librarianship or nursing.

While it is clear that the quest for professional status is motivated by a concern over a lack of esteem accorded to the female-intensive fields, it is not clear whether the professionalism model is an appropriate one to which these occupations should aspire. Furthermore, as will be shown in the following chapters, it is not at all clear that occupations, such as librarianship, gain any particular advantage in the status race when they reshape themselves by acquiring the attributes of the traditional professions.

CHAPTER 2

The Struggle for Control

In the drive to achieve professional status for their occupations, librarians, nurses, and social workers often find themselves in a quandary over territory. Establishing a unique occupational domain, that is, defining what it is that librarians, nurses, or social workers actually do and how their work differs from that undertaken in other fields, is seen by many to be an essential first step for occupations wishing to share their claim to the privileged turf of the professions. As Colson (1980) put it,

> what is there about a librarian's work that is unique, and so distinguishes it from other occupations that preparation for the work must be obtained in a unique program? What, for example, distinguishes the work of some librarians from clerks (or department heads, or ultimately, owners) in a bookstore? (p. 95)

Unfortunately, Colson along with several others arrived at the somewhat gloomy conclusion that "the work of the librarian is not necessarily identifiable as such" (p. 96). Similarly, Goode (1961) and North (1977) were of the opinion that librarians have not been successful in establishing control over a particular domain of knowledge. As Reeves (1980) observed,

> the occupation utilizes the knowledge bases of nonlibrarians, blurs lines of jurisdication that might distinguish librarians from nonlibrarians, and fails to demarcate a theoretical domain reserved solely for librarians. (p. 5)

Similar difficulties in establishing a unique identity have plagued nurses to the point where the domain problem is seen as "a major barrier to full implementation of nursing expertise" (Weiss, 1983, p. 133). In fact, Weiss found that when asked to identify the areas of medical practice that were the particular domain of nurses or physicians, nurses, physicians, and health care consumers did not identify *any* behavior as a unique nursing responsibility. Even among nurses there was

> no consensus over any behavior belonging uniquely within the nursing domain. Nurses even defined one professional responsibility as the physician's domain that physicians and consumers considered to be an area of common practice [for both physicians and nurses]. (p. 138)

Home economists, too, see the failure to agree upon the nature and purpose of their occupation as a major contributor to the field's identity crisis. In fact, MacCleave-Frazier and Murray (1984) suggested that home economics "lacks a unifying framework which integrates professional involvement over time, place, and role" (p. 69) and that reconceptualizing "its content, processes, and goals will be central to its relevance in the future" (p. 73).

Much of this concern over role clarity is the result of pressure from other, more powerful professions that encroach upon and thereby limit the activities of those in the female-intensive fields. In social work, for instance, Carrigan (1978) noted that because of the high status of the medical profession

> it becomes extremely important for social workers to do a better job of communicating their present practice and their expectations for practice to both physicians and nurses. It is these professionals who define what social workers can and cannot do in medical settings. (p. 158)

Although the question of defining a unique domain will continue to haunt the female-intensive professions for some time, it is important to note that territorial disputes are not limited to these fields. When one looks closely at the male professions of medicine, law, and engineering, it is quite evident that they too face territorial encroachment from other aspiring occupations, such as chiropractors, midwives, nurses, professional administrators, and paraprofessionals of various descriptions. However, the male professions have at their disposal more powerful mechanisms for fending off such incursions than are available, at present, to the women's fields.

AUTONOMY AND BUREAUCRACY

The interests of outside groups in the operation of the female-intensive fields can be seen in the very structures of these fields; structures that enable others, usually men, to exercise considerable control. Most nurses, librarians, and social workers carry out their practice within the bureaucratic structure of hospitals, libraries, or government agencies. As a result, some analysts argue, these occupations are unable to offer their members much autonomy. This is significant for adherents to the trait theory of professionalism because, as noted in Chapter 1, autonomy in the practice of work is usually considered to be an important professional attribute. As Simpson and Simpson (1969) explained,

> semi-professional organizations are more bureaucratic than professional ones. Instead of the control by autonomous groups of colleagues which one finds in the law firm or the university, a predominantly bureaucratic control pattern is evident in nursing services, libraries, and social work agencies. (p. 196)

The "female personality" has been used an an explanation for the bureaucratic structures that characterize the female-intensive occupations. Again, according to Simpson and Simpson (Ibid.), because

> a woman's primary attachment is to the family role; women are therefore less intrinsically committed to work than men and less likely to maintain a high level of specialized knowledge. Because their work motives are more utilitarian and less intrinsically task-oriented than those of men, they may require more control. (p. 199)

Therefore, it is argued, the female-intensive occupations are arranged in such a way as to allow women relatively little autonomy. Garrison (1979) echoed this point when she noted that

> the prevalence of women in library work... served to strengthen a non-professional bureaucratic system of control that gave the worker little autonomy. In librarianship, as in teaching and social work, the presence of women made more likely the development of an authoritative administrative structure with a stress on rules and generally established principles to control the activities of employees.... Within librarianship and other feminized occupations, compliance with sex roles prevented women from assuming much autonomy. (p. 194)

Apparently, however, Garrison, as well as Simpson and Simpson, did not consider a competing explanation for this phenomenon, that is, "that women have been recruited to librarianship precisely to accommodate a hierarchical structure, which relies on large numbers of subordinates" (Schiller, 1974, p. 129). Similarly, Bem (1983) argued that in nursing

> sex stereotypes have played a major role in leading doctors and hospital administrators to construct a work environment for female nurses that is quite

different from the work environment that they would have constructed had most nurses been male, a working environment where: (a) the physician has total authority with respect to patient care; (b) the nurse is expected to follow the physician's orders without question; (c) nurses have no self-governance; (d) nurses have no serious possibility for advancement in either status or salary; (e) nurses's services are invisible during billing, and hence, nurses are not reimbursed directly for their professional services; (f) nurses are given little or no possibility for independence, creativity, or autonomy. (p. 43)

Furthermore, there is also some question as to whether or not the female-intensive occupations are more bureaucratized than the male professions. Larson (1977), for instance, claimed that

all professions are, today, bureaucratized to a greater or lesser extent. Organizational professions should not be seen, therefore, as sharply distinct from older and more independent professions, but as clearer manifestations of tendencies also contained within them. (p. 179)

If it is true that all the professions are becoming bureaucratized, what is there to distinguish between the higher status male professions and the lower status female professions? Once again, the issue comes back to control. In both nursing and social work, practitioners often find that their autonomy is jeopardized not so much by the bureaucratic arrangement of their workplace as much as by the challenge to their knowledge base or intellectual domain on the part of higher status professionals, especially physicians. For example, physicians are seen to be experts with respect to nursing knowledge, although nurses are certainly not seen to be experts in the domain of physicians. In an analysis of court decisions involving nursing, Murphy (1987) found that the jurisdiction of nurses over a particular body of knowledge is not recognized consistently in the courts. She reported that

until recently the courts implied that physicians not only possessed nursing knowledge, but possessed it to a superior degree. The ability of the physician to testify to nursing knowledge is rarely questioned and even when questioned, it has been allowed. (p. 15)

Just as physicians often oversee the work of nurses and social workers in hospital settings, in libraries, outside "experts" are often imported to assume senior administrative positions. In fact, "the most prestigious positions in the profession frequently are held by persons who do not have our own 'professional' degree" (McDermott, 1984, p. 21). The position of National Librarian of Canada, for instance, was only filled by a librarian when the position most recently became vacant in 1984. Prior to the appointment of Marianne Scott (unusual in that not only is she a librarian but a woman, too), the post had never been filled by a professionally educated librarian. Similarly, the director of the New York Public Library is not a librarian, nor is the Librarian of Congress, arguably *the* most senior library position in the world.

The perception of librarians' skills (or lack thereof) is nowhere better illustrated than in the rationale given by those (usually men) who appoint outsiders (usually men) to these exalted posts. For example, James Billington, who was appointed as the 13th Librarian of Congress in 1987, is an historian who holds no professional library degree. During the meetings of the U.S. Senate Rules and Administration Committee prior to his appointment, Representative Claiborne Pell argued that although librarians "consistently made an excellent case for bringing professional training and experience in library management to this important position," the office of Librarian of Congress has "become a position of such influence in the world of scholarship and letters that it requires a special breadth of vision and intellect, without which a technical competence alone simply would not suffice" (Nelson, 1987, p. 4). Clearly, Pell's argument suggests not only a blatant disregard for the professional qualifications of librarianship and ignores the scholarship of a great many gifted librarians, but it reflects a basic lack of respect for the abilities of those who have chosen to work in this field. Similarly, following the appointment of Timothy Healy (a Jesuit priest) as director of the New York Public Library in 1989, one of the appointing trustees indicated that *none* of the several short-listed candidates for the position held the M.L.S. degree (Kniffel, 1989).

The appointment of men, whether or not they are trained librarians, to the top positions in the field of librarianship is nothing new. In fact, the male control of librarianship is the result of "a vigorous policy of male recruitment" which came about, according to Hildenbrand (1985), because "it came to be widely believed that the best way for a man to be assured of advancement was to enter a women's field, and many men entering the female-intensive professions anticipated managerial careers" (p. 190). Indeed, Keyes D. Metcalf and Edwin Hatfield Anderson "believed that although libraries needed to pay higher salaries to attract more qualified competent staff members, salaries would not drastically increase until more men were attracted to a female-dominanted profession" (Hernon, 1983, p. 221). In fact, it was this principle that guided the hiring practices at the New York Public Library during the 1920s and 1930s.

The same thing occurred in social work into which men were heavily recruited on the assumption that they would improve the status of the field. As a result they held (and continue to hold) many of the best paid and most prestigious positions in the field within a relatively short period of time after they entered the occupation (see, for example, Chafetz,

1972; Fortune and Hanks, 1988). According to Bernard (1983), home economists, too,

> tried the same ploy. Some even changed the name of their departments or schools to get rid of the female stigma. Again the top positions passed into male hands. The influx of men into the teaching profession has had a similar result. . . . So the pay and prestige of the higher positions are improved but the lower echelons, primarily female, remain far behind. (p. 30)

PERCEPTIONS OF THE FEMALE FIELDS

With the exception of the highest status positions, that is, those that are often filled by men, there is little value assigned to most of the jobs undertaken in the female-intensive fields. One of the major reasons for this is that it is widely assumed that women's work can be done by anyone because it requires little in the way of special skills. As Hildenbrand (1989b) pointed out, the most striking fact about the women's fields is that "the work of the entire profession is devalued or perceived to involve less skills and intellectual effort than it actually does" (p. 208).

Several studies of librarianship support Hildenbrand's argument. In an investigation of the public's perceptions of the work of librarians and lawyers, Harris and Sue-Chan (1988) found that public library users and university students underestimated librarians' level of involvement in administrative and technical tasks, whereas they exaggerated the skills involved in practicing law. In addition, both groups of subjects perceived lawyers to be significantly more intelligent that librarians. Male respondents, especially, had a tendency "to emphasize the clerical aspects of library work and to underestimate the educational requirements of librarianship" (p. 95). Similarly, in Edwards's (1989) study of school principals (the majority of whom were men), most overestimated the amount of time school librarians spent on clerical tasks and underestimated their involvement in teaching.

In a study of university faculty members' perceptions of librarians, Divay, Ducas, and Michaud-Oystryk (1987) reported that the faculty viewed librarians primarily in a service role within the university and did not perceive them to have much to do with management, teaching, or research (functions which most academic librarians see as central to their jobs). In fact, several faculty members who participated in the study reported having had contact with librarians who worked in the circulation or interlibrary loan departments of the university library system; departments which are *not* staffed by librarians (instead, these types of operations are normally carried out by clerical and paraprofessional workers).

The results of these studies reveal that judgments about librarians reflect not only a lack of understanding about who librarians are vis-à-vis other library staff, but a misunderstanding about the nature of the work they perform. In particular, there is a tendency to see the work as being primarily of a clerical nature rather than possessing "professional" elements. Similar findings have been reported in nursing studies. For instance, Webster (1985) found that medical students tend "to lump all nonphysicians into the category of nurse" (p. 316) and that male students, in particular, tend to view the work of nurses as talking to patients, "scut work," or "dirty stuff," such as keeping patients clean and looking after bed pans. Just as was the case with librarianship, these activities are normally performed by hospital staff other than nurses.

One question arising from all this is whether the general public really understands the work of the higher status occupations any better than they understand the work undertaken in the female-intensive occupations. Certainly in the Harris and Sue-Chan study (1988) the work undertaken in the high prestige occupation of law was not very clearly understood by the participants. However, their "perceptions of law were unrealistically flattering and their perceptions of librarianship exaggerated its low status" (p. 106). This study suggests that while the public may have a generally poor understanding of what takes place in most occupations, their ideas about the traditionally male professions may reflect a sort of prestige "halo," while the reverse is true of their views about the female-intensive professions.

Anyone Can Do Women's Work

It is widely assumed that nearly anyone can turn a person over in bed, check out a book, or talk to someone who is unhappy. Although this is true, these assumptions, when applied to librarianship, nursing, and social work not only greatly oversimplify the actual nature of the work undertaken in these fields, but serve to maintain the idea that this type of work is of little worth. Lewis (1977) argued, for example, that,

> to the extent... that nursing is viewed as a kind of professionalized female-ness, it is bound to be perceived as not quite the same thing as work, both in the eyes of the general public and in the presumably more enlightened vision of feminists. In the first case the correspondence between characteristics of nursing and conventional expectations for feminine behavior makes nursing an acceptable occupation for women. In the second case it is this very acceptability and nursing's apparent failure to assault the limitations of ascribed sex roles, that label it an unworthy alternative for women who seek to elevate the status of their sex. (p. 91)

As a result of this devaluing process, when the members of the women's professions wish to enhance their status in the eyes of others, they often emphasize only those aspects of their work that are easily recognized to be difficult and demanding, while at the same time de-emphasizing those aspects which involve service, that is, the "easy" jobs. Tasks that involve administration, the operation of technically sophisticated equipment, or carrying out research are usually seen to be jobs that cannot be done by "just anybody." And, typically, these are the very types of activities that are usually undertaken by men.

In social work, for instance, steps taken toward the goal of "professionalization," that is, changes undertaken to make the field "more intellectual, rational, scientific, and administrative—in short to give it 'male' qualities," can seen as part of an effort to "defeminize" this occupation (Chafetz, 1972, p. 18). In other words, professionalization, by definition, seems to be a process whereby an occupational group assumes a male identity by promoting the type of work normally done by men and by distancing itself from its connection with women through the devaluing of women's work. According to Hearn (1982), "full professionalization comes when the activity is fully dominated by men—in both management and the ranks. It is the fate that awaits the semi-professions" (p. 195).

It would appear then, that one of the unfortuntate byproducts of professionalization is that it may inevitably lead to a deemphasis or denigration of those aspects of the female-intensive occupations that involve service and personal contact.[1] One illustration of this can be found in Garrison's (1979) disdainful observations about librarians who attempt to be helpful to their patrons:

> In established professions, the practitioner supposedly assumes the responsibility for deciding what is best for the client. Whether or not the client agrees is theoretically not a factor in the professional's decision. Thus a doctor does not generally give whatever treatment the patients requests, but prescribes what he or she thinks is correct. In contrast, librarians tend to 'serve' the reader.... the passive, inoffensive 'service' provided by the librarian is... a natural acting-out of the docile behavioral role that females have traditionally assumed in the culture. (p. 189)

Lack of Compensation for Women's Work

The idea that anyone can perform the service functions that are carried out in the female-intensive occupations, and that these functions are

---

[1] Ironically, of course, this very service orientation for which the women's professions are devalued is considered to be an important professional attribute by most trait theorists but only, apparently, when applied to the male professions.

somehow natural to women, has resulted in the low rates of pay which are endemic in these fields. As Mauksch and Campbell (1985) explained,

> when women are defined as expressing their natural needs and talents in their work, the rules of the marketplace can be reinterpreted. Since economic rewards must be less important to people who are doing what comes naturally, the rules of contract change. (p. 227)

Not only do the rules of contract change when considering the exchange of wages for service in a woman's field, but so, evidently, does the notion of morality. For example, Chapman (1985) noted that in the case of nursing "goodness and mercy seem to be inextricably linked with chastity, poverty and obedience" (p. 43). Furthermore, she suggested, there seems to be a fear that "if the financial rewards become too high, young people will be attracted to nursing for the wrong reasons. Desire to serve humanity will take second place to avarice" (p. 43). Not surprisingly, many members of the female-intensive professions object to the idea that their services are not worth paying for. In fact, as Bernard (1983) pointed out,

> a wide gamut of primarily female professions is now in the process of challenging this image of women as naturally serving people and hence not really needing to be paid well—if at all—for what they do. (p. 31)

Nurses, in particular, have become increasingly militant in their efforts to achieve a more equitable rate of compensation. Their anger is fueled by increasing levels of disparity between their earnings and those of other health care professionals. To give just one of many possible examples, Curran and Winder (1985) reported that while nurses earned 33% of physicians' salaries in 1945, by 1985 this figure had dropped to less than 20%. As a result of this (as well as because of a great deal of dissatisfaction in the profession over working conditions), many nurses have chosen to leave the field in order to pursue more lucrative occupations. And of those who have continued in nursing, more and more are looking to pursue careers in public health and education. Although moving into these alternative settings does not necessarily lead to greater financial compensation, they are often seen as desirable alternatives to hospitals (which are dominated by male physicians and administrators) because they offer an opportunity for greater autonomy in practice (Bernard, 1983).

THE ALLURE OF SCIENCE

The exclusion of the female-intensive fields from Goode's (1969) list of the true professions was based largely on what he and others saw as the failure of these occupations to achieve a sufficiently developed, abstract base of knowledge. This knowledge base, according to the trait theorists, is one of the most important attributes of a profession. Thus, Rossi (1961) argued that librarians are not members of the professional elite because they "share with teachers and advertising personnel the characteristics of being close to the intellectual life, but not in it" (p. 38). Such observations, echoed again and again in the literatures of nursing, social work, and librarianship, have resulted in a flurry of research activity in these occupations which was expected to enhance their status and secure their place among the professions. However, far from achieving this goal, the research itself has become a target of criticism and continues to supply a justification for trait theorists to exclude these fields from the ranks of the true professions.

Highly critical of the research undertaken in library science, Harris (1986) referred to it as largely "bankrupt," while McDermott (1984) suggested that

> there are some within the profession, and many outside of it, who would argue that library science is not a true academic discipline at all, that librarianship deals with techniques and methods, rather than being a field of endeavor which makes original contributions to scholarship and the advancement of learning. (p. 20)

Such a lament is, of course, not unique to librarianship. In nursing, too, Fawcett (1984) suggested that the field "will advance only through continuous and systematic development of nursing knowledge" (p. 84), while Brodie (1988) argued that "the lack of clinical nursing research impoverishes the education of nursing students and compromises the professional status of nursing" (p. 325).

There is an ongoing emphasis in the female-intensive fields on using research to attain greater status and legitimacy in the eyes of other more powerful professional groups. For instance, Garrison (1979) suggested that librarians perceive their low status to be due to

> the lack of a scientifically based abstract body of knowledge, the public's lack of differentiation between the "professional" librarian and the library clerk, and the inherently weak position of the librarian as implementor rather than creator of intellectual and cultural advance. (p. 189)

Thus, she argued, improving the status of librarianship depends on establishing it "on a scientifically oriented, abstract-knowledge base" (p. 189). Katz (1969) made a similar argument about nursing, suggesting that in this field, too, research is necessary to establish it as a "full-fledged profession" (p. 63). Twenty years later, Brodie (1988) emphasized the same point when she observed that the state of research in nursing enforces the belief among many health care colleagues, especially physicians, that nursing does not have a scientific basis and, therefore, should be subservient to medicine. This sense of subservience is expressed in the research policies of agencies that demand that nurse researchers seek permission from the physicians responsible for the patients' care before they can begin a study. Finally, this lack of a nursing research heritage encourages society to believe that only medical research has legitimacy and thus, it alone has a claim to public and private research funds. (p. 325)

In response to this image Hinshaw (1983) suggested that nurses should market themselves as "nurse researchers" in order to create a public perception of nurses as scientists which would thereby increase their ability to influence health care policy and maximize their share of health care resources.

Despite the criticisms levied against nursing research, there is some evidence that the questions asked by nurse researchers are of a different nature than those asked by physicians. According to Larson (1984), nurses are "concerned much less with pathology than they are with a person's ability to function and be productive" (p. 132), thus

the physician seeks to diagnose and, when possible, treat a pathological syndrome. Nurses, in addition to carrying out the therapeutic regimen prescribed by the physician, seek ways to help the healthy individual maintain the best physical and mental status possible. (p. 132)

Based on this difference in orientation, Larson made the perhaps optimistic prediction that as the public becomes more aware that much of the very expensive biotechnical research undertaken by physicians is useful only in diagnosing rather than in curing disease, the preventative orientation of nursing research will be increasingly valued.

The perceived connection between enhanced status and the conduct of research is also evident in the social work literature. For instance, Euster (1980) observed that

despite a pessimistic projection of their relative standing in the professional and university hierarchies, social work faculty suggested that increased research, publications and knowledge-building activities may serve to enhance their image and credibility in the more traditional university community of scholars. (p. 13)

This is not always a matter of choice, of course. As is true in nursing faculties and library schools, many faculties responsible for the education of social workers are under considerable pressure by their host institutions to "buttress the science base" (Geismar, 1984, p. 135).

In all the female-intensive professions, the concern over a lack of scientific rigor and the slow development of a unique base of knowledge is normally discussed in relation to the more powerful male professions. In librarianship, for example, Reeves (1980) claimed that "the policies and standards articulated by library associations and schools do not have the abstractness and logical rigor associated with the established professions of medicine, law, or theology" (p. 5). Similarly in nursing, Hinshaw (1983) argued that the image of research "is basic to the credibility of the discipline's decision processes" (p. 2), particularly if nurses hope to influence health care policy or "function in the ranks of major decision makers" (p. 2).

Conducting research in order to enhance status and credibility and, in particular, undertaking research as a way of imitating the male professions has caused some members of the female-intensive fields to pause and reflect on the implications of such pursuits. Welch (1980) observed, for instance, that

> nursing acknowledges its caring functions but sees them as subordinate to the scientific process—that is, to rational ways of thinking, which are usually associated with masculine traits. Although the influence of sex-role stereotypes on the profession has begun to be recognized, nursing continues to act as if it cannot gain status without adopting male role stereotypes. (p. 724)

Critical of the research emphases in social work, Humphreys and Dinerman (1984) noted that not only has "the increased technical sophistication of research left the bulk of the profession behind as practitioners increasingly found research irrelevant or incomprehensible" (p. 195), but that researchers in academic settings are perceived by those in the field to be isolated from the problems and concerns of practitioners.

Even the methods of science employed in the research carried out in the female-intensive disciplines (empiricism as opposed to qualitative methods) have been criticized. The choice of these methods are seen by some to reflect what are primarily political motivations for research rather than any real interest in the phenomena being studied. For instance, Bennett (1988) observed that "librarians have fully adopted an external, positivist model of the physical sciences as the exemplar of truth and academic respectability" (p. 18), while Harris (1986) berated library and information science researchers for making a "fetish" of certain methodological approaches and, as a result, ignoring significant questions in the field. Similarly, Karger (1983) claimed that in social work, a good deal of "scientism" is simply an attempt on the part of academics to establish control over the field:

> it is a struggle between the researcher-academicians and practitioners for control of social work. . .it is a struggle for who controls and defines the profession and, subsequently, who accrues the status associated with that leadership. (p. 202)

Home economists, too, have been taken to task for overemphasizing science and empiricism as a means of boosting the occupation's status. According to Vincenti (1982),

a consequence of the profession's disproportionate loyalty to empiricism and the related emphasis on specialization has been to weaken the integrative, holistic perspective of home economics which is nececssary to help people deal with problems as they live them in families. (p. 240)

WHAT'S IN A NAME?

Nowhere is the notion that science is the cornerstone of professional status better illustrated than in the controversy in librarianship over the name of the field. As Bennett (1988) pointed out, "librarians recognize their status, do not like it, and are (and have been) struggling to find ways out of it" (p. 180). One manifestation of this struggle is the various strategies used by members of the field to avoid being identified with the library profession. One of these strategies is to give a new name to librarianship. For instance, aspiring entrepreneurs in the information brokerage business have been advised to refer to themselves as "consultants" because, according to O'Leary (1987), "if you call yourself a librarian you're lessening your value" (p. 28).

The need to escape from the label of librarianship, coupled with a preoccupation about the status of science, was at the root of the decision of many North American library schools during the late 1960s and early 1970s to change their names to include the term "information science." Despite the widespread use of this term, however, considerable confusion remains about exactly what distinguishes librarianship or library science from information science. According to Bennett (1988),

much of the work done by persons who called themselves documentalists... information scientists, and...managers of information systems is similar if not exactly the same as library work. (p. 80)

Given the difficulty of separating library science from information science, it is interesting to consider the development of master's level programs in information science in some of the North American library schools. One such program which leads to an M.I.S. degree is designed to

combine knowledge of computing and communication technology with an emphasis on the content of information systems and on the needs and behavioural patterns of the users of information systems. (University of Toronto, 1989, p. 20)

One has to wonder what the future will hold for such programs since, according to many in the information field, library science remains virtually indistinguishable from information science.

In an historical overview of the labels used in the field of librarianship, Shapiro (1984) observed that with the founding of an Institute of Information Scientists in Britain,

> an important step in terminological social-climbing had been taken. Information retrieval was now claimed to be a *science*, practiced by *information scientists*, whereas the practitioners of "library science" had never taken their science seriously enough to call themselves *library scientists*. (p. 118)

Shapiro (Ibid.) noted further that

> library work may be labelled *information science* if this will upgrade the profession's image, but the *information scientist* will really be a librarian with new tools. (p. 120)

Men have been found to be particularly evasive about telling others they are librarians, opting instead "for a more gender-neutral or masculine professional title, such as educator or information scientist" (Morrisey and Case, 1988, p. 454). In fact, this rather well-known tendency in the field led Gorman (1990) to quip that information science is simply "librarianship practiced by men" (p. 463).

It would seem then that in the opinion of many writers, information science is simply an illusion which, as Bennett (1988) put it,

> promises to make librarians into scholars, to allow them to escape the stigma of librarianship and libraries, to permit them to join a male-dominated province, and clearly to enable them to partake of academic research. (p. 110)

Thus, the attraction of information science for many in the library profession lies not so much in its somewhat difficult-to-delineate domain of knowledge, but rather that it carries with it the status of science. Even more than that, however, the prestige represented by scientific research derives from the fact that it is perceived as a male preserve.

As noted earlier, that which is stigmatized and not valued in librarianship (as well as in nursing, social work, and the other female-intensive fields) arises from its identity as a female pursuit. Recognizing the futility of trying to create a new male science from a longstanding female occupation, Gorman (1990) suggested that it is time for librarians "to recognize and proclaim that there is a body of knowledge called librarianship, that it has value and coherence" (p. 463). Despite the good sense in Gorman's advice, however, it may be dangerous to pursue such a reasonable tack in what is still very much a male world. For instance, in the appraisal that resulted in the recent closure of the library school at Columbia University, one criticism levied against the school was that its concentration on bibliographic control, that is, traditional librarianship, was outdated and "out of sync" with the modern emphasis on information science. Thus, failing to recognize how others outside the field see and assign value to areas of study may be a recipe for disaster.

The criticisms directed against Columbia's library school are interesting to consider in light of the developments taking place in other university departments at this time. According to Hayes (1988),

> schools of engineering have established departments of 'information science' as well as of 'computer and information science.' Schools of business or management almost uniformly have information systems departments. Schools of medicine have programs in 'medical informatics.' Many universities are creating academic units encompassing the cognitive sciences. Law schools have a legitimate claim on copyright, and economics departments on the economics of information. In other words, schools of library and information science are not alone in establishing a role in the 'information society,' nor are they the only academic programs providing education for information professionals. (p. 47)

The widespread use of the term "information science" rather than "library science" to describe these new initiatives in the traditionally male disciplines of business, medicine, and engineering is not coincidental. First, most people in these departments have little, if any, knowledge of the extensive overlap between library and information science. Second, even if it were apparent that most of the skills being imparted in these programs have comprised the core of the knowledge base of librarianship for many years, the title of "librarian" is hardly likely to appeal to the graduates of such programs for the simple reason that it implies that they are skilled only in women's work. Thus, introducing the "new" field of information science into male curricula is a way of legitimizing what have, in the past, been seen as women's skills.

FACULTY STATUS FOR LIBRARIANS

Librarians who work in academic settings have been particularly likely to emphasize the importance of research as the key to gaining respectability and status.[2] However, despite their efforts, most university faculty

---

[2] It is probably not coincidental to this phenomenon that a disproportionate number of academic librarians are men.

members do not regard their colleagues in the library as true academics or "real" faculty, regardless of the number of articles they publish or their status in collective bargaining arrangements. Bennett's (1988) explanation is that librarians

> are short-changed in the academic reward systems because they are neither faculty nor staff, and perhaps because they often perform work that is invisible to the members of their institution. (p. 173)

One result of the uneasy relationship between academic librarians and their host institutions is the large body of literature that has been written on the question of faculty status for librarians. In a review of the history of librarians' struggle to increase their status in academe, Werrell and Sullivan (1987) observed that, from the 1940s until the present, academic librarians

> wanted to be active members of their campuses—to have a voice in academic affairs, to have the opportunity to contribute in a scholarly fashion to the academic world, and to be recognized as partners of the teaching faculty in the education of students. (p. 96)

However, despite the fact that nearly 80% of North American academic librarians have indeed achieved some form of faculty title, their status within the institution remains generally lower than that of other faculty members and their pay is "consistently at the low end of the pay scale for similarly ranked faculty at their institutions" (Ibid., p. 96).

Because of this apparent failure to achieve parity, a growing number of librarians share the opinion that the emphasis on achieving faculty status has, in fact, been a poor strategy on the part of the academic library associations, and may even have undermined the integrity of the field. As Meyer (1981) put it, "the implementation of faculty status is tantamount to leaving the profession for one of a supposedly higher status" (p. 42). In fact, Robbins-Carter, Sherrer, Jakubs, and Lowry (1985) argued that when academic librarians insist on comparing themselves with members of the university faculty

> it is as if we had no internal model, no professional definition (other than the M.L.S., and that degree is not always a consistent criterion), for what it takes, what it means to be a librarian. I would venture to say that it is a lack of confidence—maybe not always, perhaps only nagging, but persistent nonetheless—in our role and worth in the research community that drives us to seek our model in the faculty. (p. 314)

In a sense then, the academic librarians' pursuit of an identity or model outside their own profession represents an abandonment of their field.

ABANDONING A FEMALE IDENTITY

Abandoning one's field in order to attain higher status is a theme that is reflected in the literatures of all the female-intensive occupations. This theme of escape was evident, for example, in a study of the career development of baccalaureate nurses in which one of the respondents, a faculty member in a university nursing program, commented that she had "transcended nursing" and now identifies herself as a teacher (Lewin, 1977, p. 101). However, the attempt to escape from the female identity of the women's professions is not only a matter of bestowing a new title on one's work. It can also result in redefinitions of what "counts" as professional work in these occupations.

Simpson and Simpson (1969) observed that in the female-intensive fields there is

> a great emphasis on hierarchical rank with duties differentiated by level. Activities in direct pursuit of the organizational goal occur mainly at the lower levels. As one goes up the ladder, administrative tasks tend to replace the semi-professional ones. This situation is in marked contrast to that of professional organizations, where distinguished professors continue their research and where eminent physicians treat patients. One result is that the performance of the primary tasks loses prestige among semi-professionals, while supervision and administrative activities concerned with maintaining and representing the organization become the most rewarded ones. (p. 197)[3]

Increasingly, then, one finds that librarians, social workers, and nurses who wish to pursue that which is most highly rewarded in their fields must turn themselves into something other than librarians, social workers, and nurses, prompting Curtin (1979) to observe that "rather than developing as nursing professionals, professional nurses are evolving out of nursing" (p. 1).

As DeWeese (1972) pointed out, practitioners who wish to improve their occupational status have three options. They can leave their occupation for one of higher status, increase their status within the occupation, or improve the status of the occupation itself. All three of these strategies are evident in the female-intensive professions. Sadly, attempts to increase the status of these occupations have had little effect and, in some instances such as the effort to increase the status of librarianship by renaming it and emphasizing its "masculine" aspects, these strategies may, in the long run, result in a loss of identity in these professions.

---

[3] Simpson and Simpson (1969) use the term "semi-professional" to refer to the core tasks undertaken in the "semi-professions," that is, the central activities of the female-intensive professions.

CHAPTER 3

Higher Education and Licensing: Strategies for Status-seeking Occupations

In the pursuit of professional status, many occupations have used medicine and law as their models, attempting to employ control mechanisms similar to those used in these fields as a means by which to achieve comparable levels of remuneration and prestige. These mechanisms—university-based education, licensure, codes of ethics (with enforcement procedures), and specialty credentials—are used in medicine and law to control the activities of members and to set them apart from others. In other words, through such means these professions are able to maintain a unique domain of practice for lawyers and doctors vis-á-vis other occupational groups. In the female-intensive fields, these mechanisms have been employed with varying degrees of success; however, none have brought with them the magnitude of reward that had been anticipated.

EDUCATION

University-based education as a requirement for entry into an occupation is one of the most frequently cited attributes of a profession. Not surprisingly, then, education has assumed a status that is not simply related to its role in preparing an individual to practice in her or his chosen career. Rather, it has become laden with another role, that of legitimizing an occupation's pretensions toward professionalism for, as Abbott (1981) noted, "all upwardly mobile professional groups have emphasized education as a means of collective mobility" (p. 828).

As a result of its role as a status determinant, education has been at the root of considerable controversy in the female-intensive fields. Much of this controversy is centered on the two-tiered entry systems found in education for nursing, social work, and librarianship. To understand the potential for divisiveness that can be created by this strategy for achieving greater status, the case of nursing education is particularly instructive.

Nursing Education

At the turn of the century, physicians were a weak group. Their occupation was

> overcrowded and divided, insecure in its status and income, and unable to control who entered its ranks or to raise the standards of its education or practice. Moreover, its knowledge about disease and its ability to intervene successfully were not impressive. (Brodie, 1988, p. 320)

It was transformed, however, when a model of university-based graduate medical education was widely adopted. This system involved a lengthy period of study in basic science as well as clinical training after the completion of a general course of studies at the undergraduate level. Through this new educational process medical students were "socialized to view medical research as fundamental to...practice and as a valued ally in conquering disease" (Ibid., p. 322). Today, having persuaded most of North American society of the importance of their activities, physicians not only earn handsome salaries and are accorded a great deal of prestige, but they have been very successful in attacting large sums of research money to build their knowledge base, thereby enabling them to maintain their competitive edge in the health care market.

In contrast with physicians, nurses have had quite a different history. Until the 1950s, their education was obtained largely on the job—in hospitals rather than in university classrooms—and, for the most part, it was not under their control. For many years, student nurses were used as unpaid labor in hospitals. In fact, they were actually sold out into private nursing care by hospital administrators who put the money they earned into hospital operating budgets (Ashley, 1976). In many instances there was no formal training offered to these students and, not infrequently, there were not even any paid staff available to teach them.[1]

---

[1] Similarly shortchanged were students in library school programs who, in the early part of this century, received relatively little instruction. According to Garrison (1979), "the demand for a rapid production of library workers encouraged library schools to grind out graduates after only a brief course of instruction in the fundamental skills of 'library economy'" (p. 190). This was also true in social work during the 1930s when, as a result of a very heavy demand for workers, educational qualifications were sacrificed.

For many years, nursing leaders, that is, those who head up associations such as the American Nursing Association, or A.N.A., have assumed that the best route to achieving comparable status with physicians is to adopt a process of education similar to that modeled by physicians. In fact, the A.N.A. placed educational reform as the first item on its agenda, arguing that by erecting "substantial educational barriers to entering the profession" and by moving medical education into university settings the economic situation of nurses would be improved (Dolan, 1980, p. 36). However, although nursing educators themselves achieved greater status when nursing programs moved out of the hospitals and into the academic setting, the change had little overall impact on the status of the field as a whole. In other words, it did little to improve conditions for practicing nurses. Furthermore, the transition to university-based education for nurses has not been an easy one as can be seen in the bewildering array of qualifications and titles currently used to describe the members of the profession.

In the 1960s, the A.N.A. set 1985 as the target date by which baccalaureate education would be required for entry into professional practice. That goal has still not been achieved and great variation remains in the educational backgrounds and titles of practicing nurses in North America. At present, the A.N.A. supports two levels of nursing practice: a professional level and a technical (or semi-professional) level. To practice at the professional level (and to attain the title of "Registered Nurse" or R.N.) the A.N.A. maintains that the minimum requirement for licensure should be the baccalaureate degree with a major in nursing. For those practicing at the technical level (and to attain the total of "Associate Nurse), the A.N.A. argues that the licensing requirement should be an associate degree from a two-year community college progream with a major in nursing. This system has been adopted in some states; however, in many parts of the United States and Canada, graduates from two-year Associate Degree programs in community colleges, three-year hospital programs, or four-year university degree programs are all able to achieve the R.N. designation by passing an examination.

The ongoing attempts of the nursing associations to limit the R.N. designation to baccalaureate-level nurses have not only been unsuccessful, but have caused bitter divisions between diploma and university-trained nurses. Not unexpectedly, nurses with university-level training favor the baccalaureate standard arguing that it enables them to develop expanded nursing roles and achieve greater autonomy in practice (Warner, Ross, and Clark, 1988). They claim, for example, that it is unrealistic for nurses to "expect full professional status and salary without earning them in the academic world as other professionals do" (Stephany, 1985, p. 64). In fact, Stephany (Ibid.) suggested that it's precisely because we're an overwhelmingly female profession that we must be at least as well educated as the male-dominated world that rules health-care policy. (p. 64)

On the other hand, those who hold associate degrees object to what they perceive as a devaluing of their professional status and education. They object to the split between professional and technical nurses and argue that there is no evidence to support the idea that the baccalaureate-trained nurses are any better prepared or professionally superior to the graduates of the diploma or associate degree programs.

This division within the field, along with nursing's failure to achieve the level of status to which it aspires, led Dolan (1980) to conclude that the associations' decision to emphasize educational reform "was a critical misstep, [which] has not been reversed even to this day" (p. 36). Nevertheless, the goal of professional status for nursing remains the basis for the ongoing attempts to upgrade and unify the requirements for entry into practice. To this day, however, "confusion about titles and nursing education abounds" and "there still is no universal agreement regarding what a nurse or nursing is" (Warner, Ross, and Clark, 1988, p. 212). As a result, nurses must face the double bind of not only practicing "a profession without parameters" but representing within it "one of three somewhat vague yet complete sub-groups" (Coler and Sutherland, 1983, p. 224). This confusion over titles and roles is seen by many in the field to represent the major obstacle to achieving professionalization for nursing (see, for example, Welch, 1980). Indeed, Partridge (1978) concluded that

credibility will forever elude us as long as we maintain a system whereby education of two, three, four or five years' duration prepares one for a beginning position as a professional nurse. (p. 359)

Two-tiered Education in the Female-intensive Professions

Although some critics of nursing's educational crisis may think that the multiple entry points to nursing is "an unfamiliar arrangement in most other disciplines" (Welch, 1980), it is, in fact, similar in some respects to the educational systems found in both social work and librarianship. In social work, for instance, there has been a history of confusion and controversy over the roles to be played by workers with different educational backgrounds. More than 20 years ago, Scott (1969) commented on the tremendous diversity in the background preparation of social workers despite the strong efforts to regulate entry to the profession during the 1930s:

They range from the proverbial little old lady in tennis shoes, armed with good intentions and a high school diploma, ministering to the needs, as she interprets them, of her caseload, to the young man with a Ph.D. degree from a graduate school of social welfare engaged in a program of evaluative research on the merits of a new casework technique. (p. 83)

To address these problems, the Council of Social Work Education (C.S.W.E.) was formed in the United States when two competing predecessor organizations, one representing graduate schools of social work and the other undergraduate programs, merged. This merger, which took place in 1952,

> was an outgrowth of a long and at times bitter disgreement as to the proper role of undergraduate social work education and its relationship to graduate programs. (Humphreys and Dinerman, 1984, p. 188)

Despite this merger, however, it was not until 1969 that

> the members of the National Association of Social Workers (NASW) voted to admit social workers with bachelor's degrees from approved social work education programs to full membership in the professional organization. This status had formerly been reserved for practitioners with at least a master's degree in social work (MSW). This action in effect established the bachelor's degree in social work (BSW) as the educational requirement for the first level of professional social work practice. (Dyer, 1977, p. 487)

Just as the multiple entry points to nursing block its path toward professionalization, many in social work

> question the professional status of BSW workers and view the extension of such status to anyone with less than a master's degree as retarding the professionalization process and lowering the status of the profession. (Ibid., p. 487)

And, similar to the problems seen in nursing,

> opponents of full professional status for BSWs argued that, at most, the BSW should be seen as a professional or paraprofessional technician who could then be easily distinguished from MSWs. . . . The opponents and proponents agreed that the most difficult issue created by the acceptance of the BSW was that social work had two practitioner degrees with little, if any, consensus on how to differentiate or articulate them. (Humphreys and Dinerman, 1984, p. 197)

As did their colleagues in nursing, social workers determined that the best route for attaining professional status for their occupation was to opt for higher levels of education as a requirement for entry to practice. In fact, Lowe (1985) argued that since the early part of this century "striving for professional status colored all aspects of social work development" (p. 61). Just as Dolan was damning of the members of the nursing hierarchy for moving their profession in this direction, Lowe decried the choice of social workers during the 1930s to focus on education "rather than moving to exercise control over the labor that would occupy most social work roles" (p. 61). Using language that is remarkably similar to Dolan's, Lowe claimed that "this fundamental error continues to plague the profession today" (p. 61). Thus, just as is the case in nursing, the controversy over the right to practice is still very much in evidence in social work. Master's level social workers often object to the professional status accorded to holders of the B.S.W., while the B.S.W.s argue that there is little discernible difference between them.

Library Education

All this confusion over titles, boundaries, and roles is not limited just to nursing and social work. In librarianship, too, there is an ongoing conflict over educational requirements for practice. Since the time of the outspoken library educator Melvil Dewey, in the late 1800s, it has been argued that a general undergraduate education should be a prerequisite for those entering library training programs. And, since the late 1940s, professional education in this field has constituted one to two years of graduate work in library science preceded by (at least) four years of undergraduate studies.[2]

At present, about 80 percent of those who are employed as librarians in the United States have some kind of library degree or certification (Heim, 1988), leaving a significant number of people in the field who do not hold these credentials. As a general rule, most of the professional positions in larger North American libraries require the M.L.S. There are, however, two significant exceptions to this pattern. Neither the United States federal government, through the Office of Personnel Management, nor the Library of Congress require the M.L.S. for entry-level librarian positions.

Given the relatively large number of uncredentialled "librarians," it is probably not surprising that even though the model of professional training in librarianship has a long history, tensions similar to those observed in the other female-intensive fields are also evident in this field. Just as workers who have achieved the "professional" designation in nursing are at odds with those who are considered "technical" nurses, library workers who are professionally educated are occasionally in conflict with those who are considered paraprofessionals (as well as with those who may have no formal training in librarianship).

---

[2] Interestingly, all the master's level graduate programs in Canada library schools are of two years' duration, most of those in the United States take only one year to complete. This raises, of course, the interesting question as to what, precisely, is the core domain of knowledge in this field.

Much of the tension between these groups has come about as a result of a blurring of occupational roles. Due to a lack of clarity about who is responsible for what, a certain amount of belligerence has been evident on the part of nonprofessionals (both paraprofessional library technicians as well as clerical staff) about the lack of objective standards against which their level of competence can be assessed vis-á-vis that of the more highly regarded professional librarians. This argument has been fueled, in part, by employers who question the need to pay for "professional" librarians when they could install cheaper nonprofessionals such as the graduates of library technician programs. The American Library Association (A.L.A.) has attempted to respond to this by distinguishing the task domains of professional and nonprofessional library workers. Thus,

> professional work is contrasted with 'routine applications of rules' on the one hand—the task area of the library assistant, or as it is sometimes called, the library technician...and with 'supportive work'—the domain of clerical workers. (Winter, 1988, p. 89)

It is interesting to note that while at one time the A.L.A.'s emphasis was on preventing library professionals from doing nonprofessional tasks, the focus has shifted recently

> to a concern about nonprofessionals performing professional tasks. Before, carrying out nonprofessional tasks was viewed as a threat to the prestige and status of librarians. Now it seems that the threat posed by the new information technologies to the occupation's jurisdiction and dominance is considered to be of greater importance. (Reeves, 1980, p. 26)

Adding to the confusion about credentials in the library field is the ongoing discussion among library educators about the need to develop undergraduate programs in library and information science. Although suspect because they would greatly increase the potential enrollees in library school programs and, hence, assure ongoing funding for schools, some of which face termination, such programs are touted as a means by which the library field can compete with other disciplines that are cashing in on the information business (Berry, 1985).

The Value of Education for Librarianship

It is not uncommon for practicing librarians and library educators to disagree with one another about the relevance and practicality of the education being delivered in the library schools (see, for example, Lester, 1990). In fact, library education has been criticized for elitism in much the same way as baccalaureate-level nursing education. For instance, Nelson (1980) argued that much of the theoretical work being done in the library schools has been developed not so much "for the sake of advancing library work, but for the sake of passing the attribute test for professionalism" (p. 2030). And, more than 20 years ago, Stokes (1967) complained about the value of a doctorate in library science suggesting that it "springs more from a misguided sense of status than from any benefit which success in the doctoral program brings to the daily running of the library" (p. 3599).

Losing touch with professional constituencies (or, for that matter, with the demands of host universities) can be fatal to the small and vulnerable departments which house educational programs for librarians, social workers, and nurses. For instance, according to Paris (1990), since the late 1970s, 15 library schools in the United States have been closed (or are due to close). Two of the most controversial of these closures (or threatened closures) were those at Columbia University and the University of Chicago, "the country's two historically most important library schools" (Koenig, 1990, p. 723). Koenig suggested that the principal reason for the demise of these schools was that they had become too narrow in focus. Columbia failed to act on the broad hints of the university administration to become more "scientific" in orientation and became isolated from the mainstream of university activity, while the Graduate Library School at Chicago failed to make its program sufficiently attractive to students to keep up its enrollment. Ironically, these closures are happening at a time when the term "information age" is on everyone's lips. In fact, Hayes (1988) observed that while

> in virtually every library school new constituencies are being identified, beyond the historical focus on libraries. . . at the same time, many universities have considered closing their library schools. (p. 48)

TERRITORIAL ENCROACHMENT IN THE FEMALE FIELDS

The closing of the schools, along with the reshaping of library and information science programs so that they become part of other, more general, university programs, has a pattern similar to that seen in some schools of nursing. Here one finds more powerful players in the health sciences community taking over general "health care education" with the result that nursing schools are sometimes either lost or subsumed into other faculties. Indeed, much of the controversy over entry to practice in the female-intensive occupations can be seen as a struggle for control. The associations, fueled by the concerns of their most upwardly mobile members, exert pressure to increase educational standards in the hope of attaining greater prestige (and, of course, greater salaries). However, these pressures do not go unchallenged, either by the members who feel that they are likely to lose the status they have already achieved or, and perhaps more importantly, by other groups who would like to exercise control over these occupations. As Lester (1990) pointed out, this type of territorial encroachment is very much in evidence in the library and information science field:

> The territory of information science and information management is not ripe for the taking. The Computing Sciences Accreditation Board, the American Assembly of Collegiate Schools of Business, and the Accreditation Board for Engineering and Technology all have interests in and potential claims on the information science/information systems turf. (p. 584)

Paris (1990) made a similar observation noting that in the closure of some library schools, they were seen to be

> encroaching upon the pedagogical territory of other schools and departments. In particular, business, computer science, and management information systems faculty had become alarmed that MLS curricula threatened their own course offerings. . . . Information management had suddenly become valuable territory, and leaders of the larger and more powerful academic units were loath to see the library school occupy it alone. (p. 41)

What is curious about these analyses is their silence on the issue of gender. Quite obviously, the more predatory academic departments in these disputes are those in which men, traditionally, have studied. And also, quite obviously, they wield considerably more power in what Paris referred to as "turf battles" than do educators in a woman's field who have been unable "to defend their instructional domain or to explain to the satisfaction of influential outsiders what the business of education for the information professions is all about" (Paris, 1990, p. 41).

External Control Over Nursing

Fending off powerful professional groups who have an interest in colonizing the female fields is particularly well illustrated by the example of nursing. With repect to education, for instance, it is not only the non-baccalaureate nurses who are opposed to increasing the standards for entry into professional nursing practice. In a thinly disguised attempt to protect their own domains, physicians have objected to the changes proposed in nursing education. In fact, one physician went so far as to suggest that "if nurses want status, then they should become doctors"

(Draper, 1989, p. 1217) and that the field of nursing should leave room for those "with lesser ambitions."

In 1977, the Committee on Medical Education of the New York Academy of Medicine published a statement on nursing education in response to proposed changes in nursing licensure regulations in the state of New York. These changes would have amounted to a ratification of the A.N.A.'s recommendations that the R.N. designation be limited to baccalaureate-trained nurses. The Committee's statement, which condemned the proposed changes, is very much a reflection of self-interest on the part of physicians, although it was couched in terms of concern for nurses and their patients. The Committee on Medical Education (1977) noted that,

> although studies have been published by eminent nursing educators and administrators, prestigious general educators, medical administrators, deans, and sociologists, the grass roots of the nursing profession was seriously underrepresented and *the voice of an experienced practising physician was hardly ever heard*.... The committee believes that nursing education and practice, like war, are far too important to leave to nurses, administrators, educators and sociologists alone. (p. 491; emphasis mine)

Arguing that there is no evidence to suggest that a university-educated nurse is "better" than a nurse trained in the three-year hospital or diploma program, the Committee (Ibid.) suggested that transferring nursing education from the hospital to the campus would dilute the "most essential part" of the nurse's education, that is, "direct and intimate contact with patients" (p. 499). They predicted that baccalaureate-trained nurses would soon become dissatisfied with patient care and "covet duties involving only administration and supervision" (p. 494), thereby relegating traditional activities to nonprofessionals. Thus, they argued that

> nursing educators must not be permitted to forget that young people become nurses to serve others. This is and always has been the objective of almost all who become nurses. This idealistic attitude is fundamental to all health care. To lose or displace it would ill serve both profession and public. Most nurses are needed to take care of human beings, sick or well. A minority, albeit an important one, is needed for administration, teaching, research, and paper work. (p. 502)

Nursing's push for autonomy, expanded roles, and increased status has been expressly opposed by physicians who have appealed to the service ethic in order to keep the nurses in line. For instance, the Committee suggested that

> the delivery of optimum health should be a cooperative effort *under the physician's leadership, wherein nurses and other health-care personnel work*

under his supervision. An independent, autonomous nurse practitioner is inconsistent with this position and must lead to second-class medical care. (p. 502; emphasis mine)

Given this response on the part of the Academy of Medicine, it appears that the well-educated, autonomous nurse practitioner poses a serious threat to physicians for one seldom sees such a naked attempt on the part of an occupational group to maintain control over the practice of another. In fact, Keddy, Gillis, Jacobs, Burton, and Rogers (1986) warned nurses that it would be naive for them "to expect willing support from physicians because the expanding role of nursing encroaches on their territory" (p. 752). Indeed, it is worth asking whether the nurses' role is actually expanding, or whether the fight between the nurses and the physicians has more to do with merely having the nurses' actual role in the present health care system finally be acknowledged.

At odds with those who argue that well-educated nurses are likely to abandon service to their patients are those who suggest that by increasing the quality of nursing education the quality of care will also increase. For instance, Ashley (1976) suggested that

> physicians and hospital administrators, even some who are critical of our nation's health care institutions, still do not see much of a relationship between the quality of care received by patients and the education of the nurse. Some physicians still argue that hospital schools must be maintained. Although it is a crucial factor in quality care, the education of the women who give most of the care to patients most of the time has not yet received sufficient attention. The importance of quality nursing is frequently not even mentioned in discussions on health care. (p. 33)

However, arguments such as Ashley's seem to carry little weight. In the case of the nurses in New York state, the physicians' warnings appear to have carried the day. According to Dolan (1980), the proposed changes to the licensing requirements were never passed.

Overall, then, the educational strategy followed by the nursing profession to upgrade its status vis-à-vis physicians has not been altogether successful. Not only is the field divided over the appropriate criteria for entry to professional practice, but even in the pursuit of research, embraced by many nursing educators as part of an overall package for upgrading the profession, nurses have failed to match their male medical colleagues in attracting research dollars. As Brodie (1988) observed, nurses have

> struggled to obtain state licensure laws, develop professional organizations and journals, and seek help from philanthropic groups to support them in their quest for quality nursing education. Nursing's success at obtaining

philanthropic support was a dismal failure when compared with medicine"
(p. 323)

This is due, in large part, to the success physicians have had in maintaining a monopoly on what is seen by the public (as well as research funders) to be "real" medicine.

Similar issues of control have faced social work and librarianship. In psychiatric social work, for instance,

> the structure of academe in the early twentieth century was predominantly male controlled, especially at the graduate levels. Ordinarily the deans or directors of the social work schools were men who held Ph.D.'s, as they were at the Smith College School for Social Work. In the field, the practising graduates were ordinarily supervised by male M.D.s and psychiatrists, even though the predominant numbers among the social work practitioners were always women. Psychiatric social workers were never successful in challenging or changing these power relationships; as a result they never achieved the kind of internal autonomy, control of membership, and prestige that their models, the physicians, were able to garner for themselves. (Glazer and Slater, 1987, p. 169)

Thus, like nurses, psychiatric social workers have been unable to dislodge physicians from their control over the practice (and rewards) of medicine.

Similarly, academic librarians have been unable to persuade their academic colleagues to recognize them as legitimate members of university faculties. Following the professionalization model of physicians, librarians have, over the years, moved library education into the university setting, separated clerical from professional work, and advocated the importance of research. Yet, in spite of all these steps, librarians have not seen a significant increase in their status, nor have they achieved a significant measure of control over the academic environment as might be expected, for instance, if one were to see greater numbers of librarians become members of their universities' senates.

The problems faced by the female fields in exerting control over their occupations is typified by the challenges (both internal and external) to the educational standards required of their members. Control over entry to practice is, and remains, a divisive issue in nursing, social work, and librarianship. The irony in all this, of course, is that on the one hand, the female-intensive professions are castigated for their failure to exhibit "professional" attributes. Yet, on the other hand, when nurses, social workers, and librarians actively pursue the model exemplified by the traditional male professions, they are rebuked for abandoning their clients.

LEGAL CONTROLS

When occupational boundaries are blurred, governance over a field is compromised because it is difficult to exert control over who will be able to practice and by what standards they are expected to perform their duties. In the professions, entry to the field as well as standards of practice are controlled, to a large extent, by the professional schools and members' associations. This control is exercised through a combination of normative and structural mechanisms.

According to Winter (1988), normative authority is based on shared ways of thinking in a field and by professional behaviors that are acquired through the educational process and reinforced through the professional associations and the work place. Structural authority, on the other hand, is based on the "legal power with which the occupation has been vested by legislative bodies and government agencies" (Ibid., p. 59). Thus, in addition to the extended training which is normally required as a prerequisite for employment, many professions also regulate entry to employment by licensing those who meet its qualifications.

Any success the female-intensive occupations might have in achieving the status and remuneration expected by their members, while not abandoning their commitment to service, will depend on their ability to set their own agendas and control the future directions of their fields. It is not surprising, therefore, that there is a great deal of interest on the part of social workers and librarians in obtaining a legal status which would enable them to regulate entry and practice.

Typically, the type of legal status sought by these groups takes the form of either certification and title protection or licensing. Certification, which has various definitions, involves legally restricting the use of a particular title (such as "psychologist" or "librarian") to those who have met certain requirements laid down by the professional associations. Licensing is an even more powerful control mechanism whereby activities within a particular occupational domain are regulated by law, thereby limiting those who may perform such activities to holders of a license. For example, a state regulation might require that medical diagnoses be made only by licensed physicians.

According to Humphreys and Dinerman (1984), "a license to practice is generally regarded as the necessary prerequisite to full professional status" (p. 208). Furthermore,

> licensing generally requires the attainment of a certain level of professional education, an examination of competence, a periodic review and renewal, and more recently, continuing education. In addition to protecting and reserving certain practices and activities, licenses often provide for privileged

communication, for the loss of a license and proscription from further practice in the event of unprofessional or incompetent behavior or practice, and
for criminal prosecution of any who practices without a license in a licensed
profession. (Ibid., p. 208)

Although arguments in favor of licensing usually stress the need to protect the public from quacks and opportunists, the motive of self-interest
underlying the pressure to license cannot be ignored. As Iversen (1987)
observed, "although historically licensure has been touted as primarily intended to protect the client, achieving professional status seems to be the
primary intent" (p. 231). Making a similar comment about social work,
Lause (1979) noted that

> professional self-interest concerns are defined in terms of concern for public
> benefit. Creation of a licensed service monopoly, for example, is advocated
> solely in terms of consumer protection. The political and economic benefits
> to the profession itself, resulting from the control over the supply of service
> providers, constitutes a latent issue within professional discourse. (p. 549)

Thus,

> within the sociology of occupations, it is thought that the primary and most
> direct consequence of licensing is the improvement of the profession's own
> political economy" (p. 550)

Status is also the motive behind the pressure to bring about certification in
librarianship; a move that is seen to be a means by which professional
work could be distinguished from nonprofessional work and "true professional status" conferred upon librarians (Lindberg, 1990).

Trait theorists have found the female fields to be lacking in structural
controls relative to the male professions. However, nursing, librarianship,
social work, teaching, and home economics all do, in fact, restrict entry to
their fields through requirements for extended training and through attempts to regulate practice (albeit with varying degrees of success). According to Larson (1977),

> the visible characteristics of the professional phenomenon—professional asso-
> ciation, cognitive base, institutionalized training, licensing, work autonomy,
> colleague "control," code of ethics. . . . appear in various combinations in all
> the modern professions. (p. 208)

The levels of control exerted in the female-intensive professions are
often the subject of debate and the regulatory procedures that have been
instituted in these fields vary enormously from one constituency to another.

Nursing, for example, is already a licensed profession. In the province of Ontario, to become a registered nurse one must pass examinations that are held four times a year by the College of Nurses of Ontario. Furthermore,

> if hired by a hospital that has a collective agreement with the Ontario Nurses Association (the provincial union for nurses), a person must be registered within twenty-four months; failure to become registered results in dismissal. (Meltz, 1988, p. 4)

In social work, on the other hand, attempts to regulate the field are ongoing and licensure remains a major preoccupation of the associations. In fact, Humphreys and Dinerman (1984) noted that

> legal regulation became a major goal of the profession during the 1970s. No single activity has occupied more of the financial and volunteer resources of NASW than the difficult task of achieving legal regulation. (p. 208)

Part of the reason that social workers are so concerned about licensure is that they see it as an important means by which they can "protect the profession by being eroded by other professions with similar services" (Iversen, 1987, p. 231). Humphreys and Dinerman (1984) observed, in fact, that several other human service occupations, in pursuit of their own professional status, have been intruding on the traditional territory of social workers.

By 1983, 29 states in the United States had some form of legal regulation for social work; 10 were limited to title protection while the remaining states controlled social work practice through some form of licensure. In contrast, legislation to regulate social work has been slow to come in Canada. According to Yelaja (1985), "some provinces, such as Alberta in 1969, have passed legislation which permits voluntary registration of social workers but does not include standards of education or of practice" (p. 20), whereas in Ontario the Ontario College of Certified Social Workers, established in 1982, exercises considerably more control over its members including

> graduation from an acccredited school of social work and demonstrated practice competence. In addition, the College has established procedures for reviewing complaints and maintaining standards of practice. (Ibid.)

Using a somewhat different approach in regulating their membership, the American Home Economics Association (A.H.E.A.) developed an internally controlled certification program which is not regulated by statute (Myers, 1988). The A.H.E.A. plan requires that home economists complete an examination following receipt of a baccalaureate (or higher) degree in home economics in order to become certified. The certification is valid only for three years and renewal "is contingent upon completion of 75 approved professional development units within the three year period and payment of the annual maintenance fee" (Ibid., p. 21).[3]

In librarianship, complaints have often been directed against the schools and associations for failing to be sufficiently forceful in controlling the gateways to employment or in the application of standards for practice. For example, librarians have been criticized for a "lack of basic performance standards and our wishy-washy attitude toward requiring the M.L.S. for all professional positions" (Bayless, 1977, p. 1715). Claiming that librarianship will never develop into a "true" profession without a significant strengthening of its professional associations, McDermott (1984) suggested that the primary activity of the associations should be that of "setting standards for the certification of librarians" (p. 21). The principal barrier to installing these control mechanisms is, however, the ongoing difficulty of defining the field. As Dowell (1977) noted, it is "premature to try to obtain a legal basis for certification before we come to some common agreement as to what a librarian is and/or does" (p. 1721).

Nevertheless, although licensing and other forms of structural control may be in evidence somewhat less frequently in librarianship than in the other female professions, a number of efforts have been made to extend the regulation of practice beyond the level of normative authority which occurs simply by socialization into the field and standard-setting on the part of the professional associations. For example, in the 1970s the now-defunct Institute of Professional Librarians of Ontario (I.P.L.O.) pressured the provincial government to regulate the professional practice of librarianship through legislation. This effort failed because the I.P.L.O. was unable to persuade a sufficient number of librarians to join the association or to convince provincial legislators that librarians possess a unique body of knowledge that should be controlled by its own association (Mudge, 1984). Nevertheless, this attempt represented what has continued to be an interest on the part of some in the library community to impose structural controls on the field. At present, in the United States, "a number of states do certify school and public librarians" (Lindberg, 1990, p. 158). For instance, during the legislative session which ended March 13, 1990, the Indiana state legislature passed a bill authorizing the Indiana Library and Historical Board (L.H.B.), a five-member panel that includes the state librarian, to set certification fees and establish disciplinary procedures for certified librarians.

---

[3] In contrast, in the province of Alberta the provincial Home Economics Association is registered under the Professional and Occupational Associations Registration Act.

Provisions for disciplining librarians stem from existing licensing statutes for other fields and are based on the premise that the state should have the authority to revoke licenses it issues. (Licensing librarians. What Indiana gives, it can also take away, 1990, p. 285)

Under this bill, disciplinary action could be taken against librarians in the case of fraud involving the practice of professional activities, violation of rules adopted by the L.H.B., or being unfit to practice.

ACCREDITATION

In addition to legal measures, structural control in the female-intensive fields is also evident in the accrediting of educational programs. In the case of home economics, for instance, the A.H.E.A. review programs, while in social work the Council of Social Work Education (C.S.W.E.) is responsible for accrediting schools of social work. In fact, program accreditation in social work is linked to licensing requirements. In the United States, all states with licensing legislation for social workers require applicants to be graduates of C.S.W.E. accredited schools. Program accreditation performs a similar gatekeeping function in librarianship. Not only do most libraries require that candidates for professional positions hold the M.L.S., but many also stipulate that the degree must be from a school accredited by the American Library Association (the accrediting body in both the United States and Canada).

Because of the importance of accreditation as a control mechanism it, too, has become a focus of tension within the female professions. In both social work and librarianship conflicts have arisen between educators and practitioners over the composition of accrediting bodies and their respective roles in the accreditation process (Lester, 1990).

THIRD-PARTY PAYMENT

The regulation of third-party payment for service is another significant control mechanism in the professions. Under a third-party payment system clients who receive services from, for example, physicians or dentists, are able to recover the fees paid for these services from an insurance company or employer. Such payment schemes enable practitioners to bill their clients directly for service in the knowledge that they will be reimbursed.

Among the female-intensive professions, third-party payment is of particular interest to nurses and social workers. Although private and government insurance plans generally do not directly reimburse nursing services, many nurses feel that "participation in direct third-party reimbursement schemes by charging for their services directly... is key to the development of their professional identity" (Covaleski, 1981, p. 75). According to Covaleski, the primary motive behind the nurses' wish to gain access to third-party payment is that it would enable them to increase their autonomy. In other words, if nurses were able to bill patients directly for their services it would enable them not only to work independently of other health care professionals (especially physicians), but would assist them in clarifying their unique health care role in the minds of the public. Third-party payment works the same way in social work by enabling practitioners to work independently of hospitals and social service agencies.[4]

Facing social workers, nurses, and others who wish to gain access to third-party payment arrangements is, once again, the spectre of turf protection, particularly on the part of physicians. The privilege of direct client billing with compensation to the client through insurance plans is extremely attractive for it essentially guarantees business to those professions to which it applies. If nurses or social workers were able to take a share of the health service business through third-party payment they would be intruding, of course, on what has, until now, been the almost exclusive territory of physicians. Given that health care has been an extremely lucrative enterprise for physicians, it is not surprising that they have been fighting back vigorously. It is also not surprising that they have used the language of consumer protection to make their case, that is, they typically argue that if other professionals participate in third-party payment schemes, clients may not receive appropriate care.

THE IMPLICATIONS OF PROFESSIONALISM

The relentless drive to attain professional status has led some practitioners to worry that their fields are abandoning their traditional client base. Social work, for example, has been accused of "seeking a clientele with a higher standing in an effort to raise its own position in society" (Humphreys and Dinerman, 1984, p. 184), while librarians have been chided for abandoning the lower class client in the "quest for status" (Estabrook, 1981a, p. 126). Nurses, too, have been criticized for leaving their patients in the hands of paraprofessionals as they pursue other, higher status activities.

Third-party payment offers an exciting possibility for social workers and nurses who wish for independence from the traditional male bureau-

---

[4] As a result of many attempts on the part of social work associations, 15 states in the United States had laws in place by 1985 which required insurance carriers to extend vendors' rights to clinical social workers.

cracies within which they have had their practices controlled for many years. However, such a change in the financing of these professions is likely to lead to a dramatic increase in the number of social workers and nurses in private practice. As a result, skilled social workers will become more available to people who have access to insurance schemes which fund counseling services, while the less well-to-do members of society will be left served by the relatively inexperienced social workers who work in community agencies (Blumenstein, 1988). Similarly, hospitals may well become, once again, a training ground for inexperienced nurses, as the seasoned practitioners move out into the community to work as independent health care providers.

In librarianship, too, there is an ongoing interest in what is euphemistically referred to as "alternate careers" in the information field. For the most part, these career options involve the sale of information rather than the "free" dissemination of information that is the hallmark of traditional librarianship. Just as is the case with third-party payment schemes, it is possible that in their quest for autonomy and increased status, librarians may close off avenues to information that were once available to a wide spectrum of users, especially those in the lower income range.

Despite these risks, once cannot blame the members of the female-intensive fields for seeking the autonomy, respect, and financial reward they see being proffered to those who work in the traditionally male professions.

CHAPTER 4

Self-doubt and Self-blame

Many examples of self-blame and occupational denigration can be found in the literatures of the female-intensive professions and, as is demonstrated in the following passage, much of the criticism is focused not only on those who are most disadvantaged, but on the messengers who draw attention to their difficulties:

> The most puzzling and disturbing aspect of the library feminist's claim is understanding how this great majority of librarians—four out of every five—can be so held down by the small remaining percentage. This claim only strengthens the suspicion that despite what anyone says, women are more passive and less keenly professional than men. (Carey, 1979, p. 195)

As was illustrated by the feminization hypothesis described in Chapter 1, some occupational experts hold women responsible for the low status of the fields in which they work. Unfortunately, this propensity to look within rather than to the wider contexts within which these occupations operate is not restricted to sociologists and career development theorists. Instead, nurses, social workers, and librarians often blame each other for what are, in fact, externally imposed barriers to progress.

SELF-DEPRECATION IN LIBRARIANSHIP

In an ambitious content analysis of the library literature, Bennett (1988) observed what he referred to as a "mea culpa" convention in the field, that is, the "criticism of librarians, libraries, and librarianship by librarians themselves" (p. 119). This convention, which is characterized by themes of "self-doubt, of self-recrimination, [and] of escape (to other fields or to the future)" (p. 87), perpetuates librarians' subordinate status in the workplace. In one rather remarkable gesture of self-abnegation, the professional journal, *American Libraries,* recently published an item in which the author berated librarians for their professional pretensions, urging them to wake up and recognize that they are just "gofers" and claimed that this is what accounts for their low pay and why "nobody respects you" (Plaiss, 1990, p. 589). The curious thing about this piece is not so much the content, although in browsing through hundreds of articles in the occupational literature I've never encountered anything quite so vicious, but rather that the journal's editors made the decision to publish it all. Their decision is particularly startling given that this publication is "the official news medium of the American Library Association."

Plaiss's article also raises a question as to why someone would denigrate his own field in such a manner. One explanation for such behavior is offered by Wilson who argued that "librarians handle their identity, as bestowed on them by the stereotype, in the manner of a minority group" (Wilson, 1982, p. 13). She suggested that when members of a minority see themselves through the eyes of the majority, they become ashamed of their group and "ashamed to share its characteristics" (p. 36). Furthermore, she argued that it is this sense of shame that has led some librarians to deny their affiliation with the field by adopting other titles such as "bibliographer" or "information scientist."

Following a similar line of reasoning, Mauksch and Campbell (1985) suggested that

> the most pernicious and destructive consequences of socialization into the oppressed status involves the formation of a damaged self-image. The negative messages about one's fellow victims infiltrate the self-image and results in the message that one cannot really trust one's own group and that one's peers cannot be very important. (p. 225)

Thus, Plaiss's remarks might be interpreted as merely a symptom of the general malaise facing all the female-intensive fields arising from their uncertain status. And, in truth, while Plaiss's comments are particularly unpleasant, it is not all that uncommon to find other scathing commentary in the library literature. For instance, Stokes (1967) expressed the view that librarianship is a subject not even worthy of research, noting that

> try as I may, I cannot convince myself that librarianship is a subject which can usefully be pursued at a very lofty level of research. It does not lend itself to this kind of treatment unless it turns inward on itself and produces that effete and useless theorizing which has distinguished some parts of its studies. (p. 3599)

In a similar vein, Edwards (1986) made the grim observation that

> no one with any reasonably marketable subject background goes in for librarianship. . . the result is a vicious circle as . . . drifters become the next generation of boring librarians, totally devoid of the motivation to improve their drab libraries. (p. 399)[1]

The level of angst in the female-intensive fields is sometimes so extreme that, on occasion, the entire future of these occupations is cast in doubt. In home economics, for instance, Whatley (1974) referred to

> a frantic search for identity and status, a general confusion about what we are doing and what we ought to be doing, an embarrassing sense of guilt about our image, and . . . a deep questioning of the meaning of home economics and its reason for being. (p. 10)

Even more dramatic language has been used in librarianship. According to Winter (1988), "in certain circles an apocalyptic gloom prevails: librarians appear as an endangered species, and libraries as institutions on the verge of obsolescence" (p. 78).

Themes of self-blame also appear in the social work literature, leading Clearfield (1977) to remark that it

> yields an impression that the professional self-image of social workers is essentially negative. Indeed, it has been suggested that social work has a unique penchant for self-criticism. (p. 23)

To cite just one example, Specht (1972) described social work as

> an insecure profession, prone to seek alliances with others who appear to offer more security and status. It has flitted from one institutional alliance to another and from theory to theory. (p. 13)

ANXIETIES OVER DOMAIN

This type of self-criticism is often the result of an uneasiness over work roles stemming from the perennial question of occupational domain. In nursing, for example, Mauksch and Campbell (1985) suggested that the

---

[1] It is interesting to note that Plaiss, Stokes, and Edwards are all men, lending some support to Wilson's observation that much of the anxiety over the status of librarianship is expressed by the men in the field.

most significant aspect of the occupational stereotype that needs to be remedied "is the perception that what nurses do falls within the medical domain and represents essentially the performance of delegated and trans-ferred activities" (p. 223). This view of nursing persists in spite of evidence to suggest that nurses "do indeed perform activities that are distinct from those performed by physicians" (Ibid.) and that even when they are under-taking similar tasks, their objectives and use of information is unique.

Nursing's claim to a unique occupational domain remains the subject of much internal debate within the field. For instance, Coler and Sutherland (1983) reported that "there is still no universal agreement regarding what a nurse or nursing is" (p. 224), while Andreoli, Carollo, and Pottage (1988) have been critical of nursing for failing to define itself and its "product." In the face of this internal strife, Duxbury (1983) warned that the "unique-ness" of the field is being eroded as other health care providers are increas-ingly offering services that were once "the domain of nursing" (p. 38).

The domain issue is even more complicated in librarianship, due, in part, to the fact that the so-called "information sector" covers a vast array of workers. According to Katz (1988), "it took more than 15 years for scholars to agree on a more or less stable definition of the information worker" (p. 4). While estimates vary depending on the definitions em-ployed, "of the 422 occupations used by the U.S. Bureau of Labor Statistics for compiling data on occupations by industry, 188 were identified . . . as information workers" (Ibid., p. 6). In fact, some estimates of the number of information workers range as high as 50 percent of the entire paid work force in the United States.

Pinning down which parts of this hugh information sector fall within the domain of librarianship is difficult. Winter (1988) suggested that "the need for access to the total of shared knowledge really calls for a separate occupation, or more exactly, a separate cluster of occupations, and these are the information fields" (p. 4). He included in these fields, among others, engineers, librarians, information scientists, indexers, and classifi-cation specialists. Within this group, the librarian's domain is

> that point in the bibliographic sector where all these aspects (of the organiza-tion of information) are mastered in order to put users in touch with the records that contain the knowledge or information they seek. To some degree, this function is shared with workers who are not necessarily called librarians, just as those workers who *are* called librarians sometimes carry out functions allotted to others. But this is a question of organizational and practical em-phasis. Mediating between the user and the public record of knowledge is the special province of the librarian. (Ibid., p 6)

Winter also explained that in order to maintain an autonomous profes-sional identity, an occupation's knowledge base must have enough indeterminacy to elude control from outside forces. Its leading ideas, its integrating principles, and its underlying values must . . . be relatively abstract and relatively complex. Yet the knowledge base must not be too indeterminate, or it loses relation to technical concerns and becomes indistinguishable from the traditional fields of liberal learning. The knowledge base must strike a difficult balance between techniques and skills on the one hand and abstract ideas on the other. (p. 70)

However, it is just this indeterminacy that, at least in Wilson's view, accounts for the low status of librarianship. She argued that the notion of information work is so vague that people form the impression that anyone can do it and, as a result, librarians enjoy little status. According to Wilson (1982),

a fundamental characteristic of information makes the field especially difficult to delimit: information is everybody's business. It is a do-it-yourself field in which everyone has some interest and everyone has some competence. (p. 181)

Reeves (1980), too, argued that failing to lay claim to a unique domain has resulted in the low status of librarianship:

Without the capacity to exercise a monopoly over the performance of certain tasks, the occupation cannot achieve the visible and distinctive attributes of status that distinguish a profession. The occupation is unable to make any claim regarding the crucial importance of its skills and knowledge to society and the individual members of society. It is unable to increase the economic well-being and thus the prestige of practitioners. (p. 7)

SELF-BLAME

While it is obvious that the whole question of domain is a matter of protecting an occupation's identity in the face of external pressures, it remains a curious feature of the female-intensive fields that the blame for their various problems continues to be focused internally. For example, nurses, frustrated by their failure to stop negative media portrayals of their occupation as well as by their low salaries and lack of status, often exhort their colleagues to shift their focus away from external barriers to advancement and back onto themselves. Strasen (1989), for instance, claimed that nurses will never achieve the professional status to which they aspire until they begin "developing positive self-concepts rather than blaming external factors" (p. 5). She even went so far as to suggest that nurses should try to visualize themselves as powerful in order to bring about a self-fulfilling prophecy of nursing as a powerful profession. Similarly, Bille (1987) not only urged nurses to become better professionals but better *individuals*. Physicians, too, have jumped on this bandwagon. For example, Herbert (1983) chided nurses for creating their own image problems and noted that

> while nurses seem determined to keep their responsibilities down among the bedpans, that is where they will stay. And that is where your image will stay as well. (p. 13)

Librarians have also been prodded to change the negative occupational stereotypes of librarianship from within the profession itself. Edwards (1989) claimed that the only way to change these stereotypes "is to effect excellence" (p. 31), while White (1986) argued that "if librarianship is to change its outside perceptions it must first change its self-perceptions" (p. 59).

Throughout these examples self-improvement is heralded as the route to success for the aspiring female-intensive professions. Clearly, the underlying message here is that the problems facing the members of these professions are largely of their own making.

SELF-IMPROVEMENT

In nursing, the recommended strategies for improving matters within the field range from articulating the nurse's role with greater clarity and practicing with "compassion, knowledge, commitment and competence" (Porter, Porter, and Lower, 1989, p. 36), to changing nurses' style of dress and speech. As these examples suggest, the tone of some of this advice is often extremely patronizing. Rinneard (1975), for instance, suggested that in order to be successful negotiators at the bargaining table, nurses should dress appropriately and not chew gum, explaining that

> dress inappropriate for the situation will present an attitude of disrespect, unconcern and poor judgment, and does not invite confidence from other members at the negotiating table. Neither does conversation which includes sarcasm, flippancy or rudeness. Chewing gum is not acceptable in a professional nurse in the performance of her duties at any time and no more acceptable at the bargaining table. (p. 64)

Again bringing up the issue of attire, Reeves, Underly, and Goddard (1983) observed that

> professional image starts in the mirror. Good grooming and a well-fitting, dignified uniform or suit will increase your own self-confidence as it builds the image of all nurses. (p. 58)

These authors also advised nurses to "avoid loud laughter, inappropriate remarks, sloppy posture, and gum chewing. . . . These behaviors all say 'unprofessional' to bystanders" (p. 58).

Such useful advice cannot always be had free of charge. Some members of the health care field are making a living by marketing what they call the "professional image." For instance, the head of a "health care consulting firm specializing in nurse marketing and hospital corporate identity" advised nurses to stop blaming others for their problems. She not only recommended that nurses "make a professional statement aligned with nurse modernization and health care savvy" by wearing "corporate uniforms," but argued that nurses who object to the notion of dressing for success create for themselves "a self-constructed image barrier" (Interview. Toward a more profitable nursing image, 1984, p. 23).

As the consultant's advice suggests, much of the material in the self-improvement genre amounts to little more than encouraging members of the female-intensive occupations to drop traditionally female behaviors in favor of more masculine or "corporate" behaviors. For instance, Bush and Kjervik (1979) recommended that nurses "give up guilt" and become more assertive, while Meade (1986) scolded nurses for being "ambivalent about wanting and retaining power" (p. 24). Similarly, Kooker (1986) argued that "for nursing's sake as well as their own, nurse managers must actively participate in the power system of the hospital corporation" by developing a "corporate nursing image." She recommended that nurses identify the stereotypes held by men about women and then adopt behaviors that counteract these stereotypes.

Adding to the confusion awash in this sea of advice (much of which is contradictory) Kooker (Ibid.) both admonished women for being too feminine to succeed and at the same time warned them against excessive masculinity. She advised nurse "executives" to "eliminate girlish femininity such as a little girl voice;" "avoid a timid, tentative walk; don't smile too much;" "keep your 'people' concerns to yourself—focus on 'what's good for the company is good for everybody';" and "dress for work not play; don't get entrapped when a man comes on to you in a sexual or flirtatious way." However, she then went on to caution nurses against being seen as "hard and cold" and to "avoid tough talk and four-letter words" (p. 53).

Despite Kooker's words of caution about becoming too manly, encouraging the members of the female-intensive fields to abandon "femininity" has been seen by many to be an important step in achieving professional status for these occupations. For instance, Sadler (1984) suggested that

> if nurses were to become a little more firm-jawed and a little less dewy-eyed, they could improve their professional status overnight. The meteoric rise of the male nurse in the nursing hierarchy during the past decade proves the point. Indeed, the future of the nursing profession appears to lie in the hand

of the male nurse. Having proved themselves to be compassionate carers—despite some early doubts from their female contemporaries—male nurses are now permanently establishing themselves as fair and effective managers, articulate speakers and astute politicians. (p. 43)

BLAMING WOMEN FOR THE STATUS
OF THE FEMALE-INTENSIVE PROFESSIONS

Sadler's (1984) admonitions are similar in tone to those which have been directed toward librarians. Critical of the whole professionalism movement in librarianship, Nelson (1980) pointed out that in order "to advance their struggle for professionalism" librarians have been urged to be more aggressive and less nurturant, "in short, more masculine" (p. 2032). This type of pressure is quite evident in Garrison's (1979) analysis of public librarianship in which she concluded that

> the negative traits for which librarians indict themselves—excessive cautiousness, avoidance of controversy, timidity, a weak orientation toward autonomy, poor business sense, tractability, overcompliance, service to the point of self-sacrifice, and willingness to submit to subordination by trustees and public—are predominantly 'feminine' traits. (p. 189)

Thus, Garrison, like Sadler, placed the blame for the problems facing the female professions squarely onto the women who populate these occupations.

For an increasing number of analysts, this view is unacceptable because it "disparages feminine qualities and elevates a masculine view of power, one that emphasizes competitiveness, domination, and control" (Benner, 1984, p. 207). According to Benner, disparaging women for what they bring to their work and encouraging them to improve themselves for the sake of their professions

> is based upon the misguided assumption that feminine values have kept women [and their fields] subservient, rather than recognizing that society's devaluing of and discrimination against women are the sources of the problem. The former view—the misguided assumption—blames the victim and promises that discrimination will stop when women abandon what they value and learn to play the power games like men do. (p. 208)

In fact, the emphasis on self-improvement in the literatures of the female-intensive professions bears a striking resemblance to the self-help or "recovery" monographs that are filling the psychology shelves in bookstores. As Lerner (1990) pointed out, the advice-giving industry, a multi-billion-dollar business, teaches us to privatize, individualize and pathologize 'women's problems,' rather than to understand these difficulties as a natural and shared outgrowth of inequality and the socially constructed fabric of work and family roles. (p. 15)

Disparaging Women and Their Service Roles

Not surprisingly, the self-help/self-blame message has produced confusion and conflict among the practitioners toward whom it has been directed. For instance, Welch (1980) noted that, in its attempts to achieve greater professional status, nursing

acknowledges its caring functions but sees them as subordinate to the scientific process—that is, to rational ways of thinking, which are usually associated with masculine traits. Although the influence of sex-role stereotypes on the profession has begun to be recognized, nursing continues to act as if it cannot gain status without adopting male role stereotypes. (p. 724)

The outcome of such conflicting demands, that is, requiring of practitioners the traditionally female behaviors associated with nurturing and caring, while at the same time disparaging them and encouraging the development of what might be seen as almost antithetical male, achievement-oriented behaviors, is a no-win situation. It cannot help but lead to uncertainty as the members of these fields must inevitably come to feel that they are not quite good enough, leading them, in turn, to experience guilt and doubt about the value of their work and, indeed, to doubt their own worth.

PROFESSIONALISM AND SELF-DOUBT

According to Dolan (1980), the ideology of professionalism, so dear to the leaders of the nursing associations, "trains nurses to blame themselves for all their problems rather than to seek to alter their work environment" (p. 50). In fact, Corley and Mauksch (1988) suggested that nurses "show the consequences of being an oppressed group" among which are self-hatred, divisiveness within the field, fear of success, and the inability to agree about what nursing is—"difficulties which have their roots in uncertainties of status" (p. 138). In the face of these difficulties, many nurses have elected to leave the field entirely. Paradoxically, then, the attempt to follow the male model of professionalism may very well result in the disintegration of this occupation.

In librarianship, too, the self-blame that seems to be associated with the pursuit of professionalism has had the same ill effects that have been evident in nursing. Bennett (1988) observed, for instance, that

> the constant return to the interpretative convention that librarians need to be 'better' people—either male, or scholarly, or researchers, or service oriented— describes a state of subordination. The constant looking to other disciplines for models and theoretical substantiation of librarianship also describes a sense of subordination. (p. 180)

As though to prove him right, White (1990) recently took aim at librarians for failing to know what they are about. "In our frenzy to promote libraries, we have lost sight of whatever purpose we once had" (p 104). He also admonished librarians for failing to adopt the professionalization model, claiming that "the library should be used on its professionals' terms or not at all" (p. 106). Raising White's ire, no doubt, are articles like one which recently appeared in *Time* magazine featuring the changing nature of public libraries. In this article, Tifft (1990) noted that public libraries not only offer users the opportunity to retrieve off-site information through the use of computers, but that they have extended their services far beyond the loan of books to include toy and tool lending as well as day shelters and after-school tutoring programs. According to White (1990), such an expansion of the library's role has "trivialized" the profession so much that the public has begun to see the library "simply as a handy place to come in out of the rain" (p. 106).

White is not alone in criticizing librarians for attempting to expand their service roles. Others have also pressed librarians to abandon non-book activities in public libraries and to deemphasize the outreach aspects of library service. Ballard (1981), for example, called for librarians to

> avoid programming and other forms of non-book activities which deflect us from our central purpose. . . Book use and book circulation is the overwhelming reason why people come to the library. . . The search for alternative activities public libraries could offer to increase their user group has been long and costly, and has failed miserably. . . Public librarians should concentrate on the 'full' ten percent who use the library, not the 'empty' ninety. (p. 77)

Nice Ladies

Underlying White's (1990) critique of public librarians is, essentially, a variation of the feminization hypothesis. To illustrate, consider the following passage of his article:

In old aircraft companies it was fashionable to turn library administration over to the widows of test pilots killed while flying company experimental models. These were generally young mothers, educationally prepared for nothing except marriage and early motherhood, who now needed a job, and the company thought it ought to be a 'nice' job in a dignified office setting that didn't require any particular skills. Aerospace companies have moved beyond this, but public libraries are still run by 'nice ladies.' (p. 264)

These comments help to bring to the fore the male and female polarities that are at the root of much of the tension in the field over image, status, and professionalism. Although White (1990) and Ballard (1981) have both taken a rather heavy-handed approach in their commentaries, there is nothing new about their criticism of librarianship's service orientation. This orientation toward service is, according to Garrison (1979), part of the field's female tradition and it is this tradition that is under attack. For instance, White (1990) observed that

when in public libraries we accept the problems of adult illiteracy or latch-key children without additional support simply because these problems are there, we carry on the tradition in which the library does whatever needs to be done, and therefore the librarians obviously become secondary . . . we may call ourselves librarians, but we really wish we were in the Peace Corps. (p. 264)

White (Ibid.) argued that this commitment to service, with or without sufficient resources, has nothing to do with librarianship and suggested that what should be emphasized instead is management, "the most important course in library education" because it teaches librarians "how to make others give you the resources you need" (p. 264). White's remarks can be interpreted as an attempt to deemphasize the female aspects of the profession (manifested in service), in favor of an emphasis on management, a more masculine pursuit.

THE UNEASINESS OF MEN IN A WOMEN'S PROFESSION

In her study of occupational stereotypes, Wilson (1982) observed that, in library literature, male librarians have a tendency to distance themselves from the field by keeping "the reader aware that they were male and the stereotype applied to women" (p. 16). McReynolds (1985a) also commented on this pattern. She noted that since the 1900s, male librarians seemed particularly anxious to sublimate the feminine side of librarianship and to stress its similarities to male-dominated professions. But try though they might, they simply could not shake their image, or their own belief in their image, as mousy people. (p. 26)

In the 1930s there was a particular sensitivity in the field over the stereotype of the librarian as "a middle-aged spinster." According to McReynolds,

in their crusade to disavow this image, librarians, male and female, betrayed a belief that there was something distasteful about women growing old, being plain, never marrying. It may not have been a concept that librarians invented, but the zeal with which they embraced it surely hindered the profession and women in it. (p. 30)

Even today, many male librarians seem to have a moody preoccupation with their image, certain that the public holds them in much more contempt than is actually the case. In a study of perceptions of male librarians, Morrisey and Case (1988) found that

male librarians and library students believed the public's image of themselves to be more submissive, meek, nervous, effeminate, reserved, following, subdued and less approachable, athletic, and attractive than the undergraduate sample actually saw them. . . . The members of the male library group felt the male librarian is looked upon negatively when he actually was looked upon quite positively by the other respondents. (p. 453)

Librarianship is not the only female-intensive occupation to exhibit symptoms of a male identity crisis. Male social workers are also reluctant, on occasion, to admit that they work in a woman's field (see, for example, Wikler, 1980). In fact, Kadushin (1976) attempted to justify the segregation in social work in which men hold a disproportionate number of higher status, managerial positions. He argued that male social workers need these male-dominated enclaves within the field in order to maintain their self-esteem. For instance, he suggested that when male social workers become managers it

mitigates a number of different problems relating to maleness in a female profession. It reduces role strain, since administrative activity is a male sex-typed task; it removes the professional from direct contact with the public, thus averting sex-typed conflicts associated with direct service;[2] it resolves problems regarding the need to accommodate to supervision by a female colleague; and it mitigates the difficulties of status inconsistency, since the administrative positions are more prestigious than others that might be accessible to the male social worker. (p. 445)

---

[2] Evidently the source of this conflict is what Kadushin (1976) refers to as the "masculine taboo on tenderness" (p. 443).

Kadushin also argued that the higher salaries earned by male social workers can be justified on the basis that

> salary levels have different economic as well as different psychological connotations for male and female social workers...salaries that are in general adequate for female are clearly inadequate for males. (p. 445)

Given the difficulties some men experience as a result of working in a female-intensive field, it is probably not surprising that the male-dominated specialties within these occupations produce a good deal of the material written on status and professionalism. Academic librarianship, for example, is an area of specialization in the field in which proportionately more men than women are employed, and, according to Wilson (1982), academic librarians are unusually preoccupied with questions of status. They perceive themselves to be not very highly regarded by people outside the profession and, as a result, in their writings they often urge their colleagues to be more professional and less passive. This type of writing, according to Bennett (1988), reflects "a desire to remove oneself from a feminized profession" (p. 161).

Academic librarians also tend to emphasize class distinctions within the field. Wilson (1982) suggested that this is because superior castes within a group emphasize their superior standing by pointing out small differences in order to set themselves apart (a phenomenon she referred to as the "narcissism of slight differences"). Among librarians, the castes recognized to be superior, such as academic librarianship, are more heavily populated by men while those seen to be inferior, such as public and school librarians, are more female-intensive.

As to whether or not the perceptions of the general status of librarianship vis-à-vis other occupations are accurate, Wilson (1982) was of the opinion that they are, indeed, "an accurate representation of reality" (p. 147). She argued that the problem of status

> does not lie with the actual prestige ranking of librarians but with the stereotype and, most especially, with self-perception, with the self-image, the minority mind set librarians have developed as a result of the stereotype. (p. 153)

This comment suggests that Wilson, like her counterparts in nursing, sees the problems besetting the field as stemming from within; the result of shortcomings in the profession itself. In fact, she claimed that any enhancement in the status of the librarianship "would require substantial change in the nature of library work, so substantial as to require greatly increased educational preparation" (p. 153). Such an analysis appears to be heavily informed by trait theory, for Wilson seems to be saying that without adopting some of the features which distinguish the male professions, librarianship cannot advance its status.

Feminist analysts caution those in the female-intensive professions against accepting such a view of themselves. From a feminist perspective, the basic problem facing the female fields is the problem of assigning value to women's work, leading one nursing activist to observe that

> because society and the health care system don't value them, nurses don't value each other. This results in nurses denying a common cause with each other, lacking pride in nursing, internalizing stress and conflict as individual problems and not supporting each other. (Thomas, 1990, p. 14)

RESOLVING THE CONFLICT
OVER THE VALUE OF WOMEN'S WORK

In order to overcome this stress and internal strife, Welch (1980) offered some advice to nurses that might well be heeded by others in the female-intensive fields. She suggested that they

> explore the ways in which sexism has stunted their professional growth, and perhaps begin to understand and overcome the self-perpetuating dysfunctional practices they employ against each other and themselves. (p. 727)

Recognizing that they have failed to achieve the rewards enjoyed by the male professions, many social workers, nurses, librarians, and others in the female fields have been looking for ways to assign blame. Some turn their anger inward, pointing accusing fingers at one another for being too feminine, too masculine, or not enough of either. Others see that the barriers to progress are externally imposed and choose to fight back or leave these professions entirely. Thus, Welch's advice underscores an important choice for those in the women's fields; that of fighting the status problem from within or taking the battle outside. The approach to be taken, of course, depends entirely on one's beliefs about the source of the difficulties facing these occupations.

At present, it is unclear which choice will win out. Some members of these fields may indeed retreat into self-blame and adopt the recovery model—trying to dress better and behave more "professionally." Others may tackle the problem by trying to reshape their occupations so that they resemble the traditional male professions. Still others may try to increase the status of their fields by pressing society to assign greater value to those very characteristics that give their professions a female identity.

Regardless of which approach is taken, the members of the female fields are in for a rough time. Self-blame takes a large personal toll and contributes to friction and mistrust among colleagues. Taking on a male identity not only threatens the core activities of the women's fields, but is unlikely to be successful. As Bernard (1981) pointed out, women may

> think like men, act like men, live by the rules of the male world. They may reject identification with other women and certainly with the female world. For all intents and purposes they are 'men.' But they are almost never truly 'in.' Almost never completely accepted. Nor does their presence change the nature, structure or functioning of the male world. Though they are in the male world in the sense that they participate in it, they are not truly 'of' it. And that is the bottom line. (p. 221)

However, the alternative to imitating the male world, that is, trying to revalue women's work, is not easy. As noted in Chapter 1, there is a reluctance in the women's fields to acknowledge that gender is relevant to the status issue. As a result, any attempt to reclaim or enliven the women's professions requires some major rethinking on the part of their members (as well as the rest of society). The scale of this rethinking is somewhat overwhelming if one considers Marshall's (1989) view that women need to be

> developing their own theories (and) reconstructing the world of knowledge... which has not only missed them out as content but has in its structures and methods also taken no account of their values. (p. 277)

For librarians interested in such a reconstruction, Nelson (1980) advised that

> if we feel that our services are not valued by society, we must try to improve our services so they will be valued. However, we must recognize that the fault may not lie all within ourselves, but may be inherent in the nature of our society. Knowledge and learning, to which we are so closely allied, are not really respected for their own sake in American society....And we are a 'woman's profession,' and as women are not valued, so librarians are not valued. We must continue working to improve the status of women in society and in librarianship. (p. 2033)

Offering somewhat similar advice to nurses, Bem (1983) suggested that without aggressive challenges to the health care system, nurses will not achieve their goals. Thus, to achieve a better work environment,

> they cannot and should not wait around for people's attitudes toward nurses to change. Rather, they must force that new work environment on the physicians and hospital administrators who appear to control virtually every aspect of their working lives. (Ibid., p. 45)

Whether or not the members of the female-intensive fields will take up these challenges remains to be seen. However, one outward-looking strategy for status enhancement that is being pursued in some of these fields is to actively campaign against media portrayals of negative occupational stereotypes. As will be seen in the next chapter, this battle has consumed a considerable amount of energy over the past two or three decades, particularly on the part of nurses.

CHAPTER 5

Image Management: Marketing the Female Professions

Dowdy spinsters shushing cowed library patrons; overbearing matrons shepherding student nurses past ogling male patients; frumpy do-gooders offering advice to the poor. These are some of the stereotypes of librarians, nurses, and social workers that, in the opinion of many members of their respective occupations, account for the low prestige accorded to these fields. As a result, nurses and others have organized media watch campaigns and countermarketing strategies in an attempt to educate the public about the true nature of the women's professions.

SEX-ROLE STEREOTYPES AND OCCUPATIONAL IMAGE

Although the particular images of these professions may vary, they are, for the most part, very much bound up in general sex role stereotypes. In librarianship the dominant image is that of "genteel traditionalism, in-effectual males and shushing spinsters" (Garrison, 1979, p. 223), while in social work most functions are perceived to be "extensions of the traditional roles of wife and mother" (Kadushin, 1976, p. 441). In nursing, too, "sex stereotypes dominate both the image and the reality" (Bem, 1983, p. 40). In fact, according to Muff (1988),

> the Mother Nature archetype is the fundamental archetype behind several nursing stereotypes because nursing is so closely connected to women. When people think of nurses, they think of women and when people think of women they think of some innate ability to nurse. (p. 44)

77

Bem (1983) went so far as to describe the public's image of nursing as

> nothing more or less than the image of woman...when people think of
> nurses they think of women and therefore interpret everything nurses need or
> want or do in terms of what a woman should need or want to do. (p. 39)

The Results of Occupational Stereotyping

The president of the Registered Nurses Association of Ontario observed
that

> what is considered men's work has traditionally been more visible, and there-
> fore more valued, than what is considered women's work.....Men are thought
> to be rational, scientific, independent, and assertive. Women are seen as intui-
> tive, dependent, emotional and passive, qualities considered less valuable.
> Nursing involves skills that are 'natural' to women, while medicine is viewed
> as scientific and rational. (Thomas, 1990, p. 14)

One result of nursing's image and the perception that it does not require
much other than innate femaleness is that it is increasingly difficult to
attract people into the profession. In fact, the field is facing declining
enrollments and serious personnel shortages. As Andreoli, Carollo, and
Pottage (1988) put it,

> nursing is simply not perceived as a high-status, powerful health profession.
> The consequences of a negative public image of nursing are substantial,
> affecting not only recruitment but also the overall ability of the profession to
> attain its goals. (p. 5)

Rayner (1984) reported that British career counsellors advise their
brightest students "that they can do better than nursing" (p. 31). What
this means, in fact, is that bright students who are interested in health
care should consider becoming physicians rather than mere nurses. Such
attitudes on the part of counsellors are probably not surprising given that
even though at least half of all health care personnel provide nursing-
related services there continues to be a general public perception "that
medicine is the same as health care and that doctors know best" (Salvage,
1983, p. 181).

In addition to affecting recruitment and retention in the nursing profession, the field's image also affects its capacity to attract the public
purse. Curran and Winder (1985) have suggested that the negative public
image of nursing is responsible for the failure of the approximately one
million registered nurses employed in U.S. hospitals ("the largest group of

health-care workers who provide 24-hour patient care coverage") to be clearly identified in the national health care budget, even though "the 450,000 practicing physicians in the United States, who average less than 2 hours each day in hospitals, account for 20% of the health-care dollar" (p. 252).

The effect of image on librarianship is that it too tends to be ignored in the budget line. In the special library situation, for instance, the library unit is funded and administered by people who tend to be quite unfamiliar with its functions. As a result of the "generally low status and unimpressive image of their occupation," librarians who work in a business environment may find that their colleagues have "a lack of faith in the library's ability to help" (Slater, 1987, p. 336). Slater also commented on what she called "corporate invisibility," noting that librarians not only

> suffer from an undesirable image, susceptible to stereotypic caricature of the buns, beads and glasses variety. They also suffer from an anaemic, low profile, shallow image. In a noisy, dynamic, complex setting, like the average firm, this can lead to virtual invisibility. (p. 336)

She concluded that underfunding, low salaries, and lack of opportunity for advancement are all the result of this image and reflect employers' perceptions of the "irrelevance or low status and value of library-information qualifications and indeed of the job itself" (p. 339).

The problem of underfunding is not confined to special libraries, but also plagues the public and academic library sectors. For example, even the prestigious Stanford University library system is expected to face budget cuts of 10 to 20 percent over the next two years, while in 1990 the San Diego Public Library faced the possibility of a whopping budget cut of 62 percent. These are only two of many possible examples which illustrate how libraries become easy targets during tough financial times. In fact, nearly every issue of *American Libraries* carries at least one article on the budget problems faced by yet another library. Such funding problems are chronic and, as such, are demoralizing to many in the field. Not surprisingly, some librarians are choosing to leave the profession. As one beleaguered cataloger wrote, "Why am I leaving the field? I'm underpaid and overworked. I don't get much respect. My work has meaning, but in today's marketplace it has little value" (Para, 1989, p. 13). Sentiments such as those no doubt contribute to the difficulties in recruitment noted by Heim (1988) who indicated that in the United States "in the present and immediate future the shortage of librarians for simple replacement needs is acute" (p. 3).

Similar to the problems facing libraries (whether they fall under the administrative rubric of municipalities, universities, governments, or businesses), social work units that are housed within large institutions also find it hard to secure the resources they need to operate effectively. As in librarianship, the difficulties facing social workers often stem from the fact that the dominant professions within the host organization and those who hold the purse strings do not understand social work functions. As a result, inadequate funding and/or inappropriate mandates for the operation of social work departments is not uncommon (Jansson and Simmons, 1986).

Home economists, too, suffer from a lack of visibility and public ignorance about their work. Inana (1984) complained, for instance, that despite extensive media coverage of educational issues, the field of home economics is rarely mentioned and, as a result, "is not perceived by the public as basic or even contributing to the development of academic skills" (p. 170).

THE MEDIA'S ROLE IN OCCUPATIONAL STEREOTYPING

Many people see the popular media as principal culprits in maintaining the public's negative stereotypes about the female-intensive professions. According to Kalisch and Kalisch (1980),

> the depiction of women by the media, including the portrayal of nurses, serves to dampen their full utilization in the economy by discouraging women's occupational aspirations and encouraging their underemployment. (p. 13)

The damaging impact of media portrayals of women's work is widely felt by the members of the female fields. Surveys of nurses repeatedly show, for instance, that among the most significant issues facing the profession are improving the public image of nursing, developing public awareness of the unique contribution nursing makes to health care, and creating public acceptance of nursing as an independent profession. Remarkably similar results have been reported in a recent survey of American Library Association's members (Wallace, 1989) and in an earlier study of home economics teachers (Whatley, 1974).

Media Watch

One manifestation of the widespread concern about media stereotyping of the women's professions is the constant media monitoring that goes on in these fields. Through columns such as "In the Media" which runs in the British journal, *Nursing Times*, "the nursing press regularly invites members of the profession to send examples of how nurses are misrepresented in the media" (Gallagher, 1987, p. 674). A regular column on image has also been running in *American Libraries* since 1985 leading Sapp (1987) to observe that

> librarians are vigilant image-watchers. Much more than members of other, more established professions, librarians feel slighted by their public image. This self-consciousness has produced a great deal of literature written on the subject; some of it detached and scientific, some of it militant and rhetorical. The American Library Association has likened its crusade against the stereo-type to a war. (p. 135)

Despite widespread use of this media watch strategy, not everyone favors this approach to fighting occupational stereotypes. Stevens (1988) examined the different ways in which image-related issues in librarianship have been dealt with by various professional journals. One of these jour-nals, in which considerable space is devoted to the image question, is edited by a person who argued that we live in an "age of image and...a bad image leads to bad treatment" (Ibid., p. 837). On the other hand, editors of journals in which little attention is paid to image told Stevens that drawing attention to occupational stereotypes has a negative rather than positive impact on the profession. This is a view which has been echoed many times. For example, McReynolds (1985b) was extremely critical of the *American Libraries* image column and called on the journal to spare its readers "from these sad little diatribes about our image" (p. 213). Based on her analysis of stereotypes in the library profession, Wilson (1982) concluded that librarians should stop writing about the negative image of the field because in so doing they are contributing to the stereo-type. She claimed that "although librarians cannot banish the stereotype completely, they can improve it by not adding to it and by not disseminat-ing it, and, most important, they can control their response to it" (p. 191).

Despite such objections, vigorous media watch campaigns continue in the female fields. One of the best illustrations of a systematic approach to monitoring media portrayals of an occupational group is in the large body of work produced by Beatrice and Philip Kalisch. Their research, which focuses on the portrayal of nurses in the popular media, has yielded num-erous examples of sex stereotyping and the marginalization of nursing in health care delivery. In one study, the Kalisches examined the images of nurses and physicians presented in novels, movies, and prime-time tele-vision produced between 1920 and 1980 (Kalisch and Kalisch, 1986). They found that the centrality of the nurses and physicians' roles had changed considerably since the 1920s with the role of nursing in sharp decline. They noted that female physicians rather than nurses are now used for more and more of the female roles in the health care genre and that relative to physicians, nurses were shown to be significantly less intelligent and rational, to exhibit less individualism, and to value scholarliness and achievement less than physician characters across all the types of entertainment media. . . . Media nurses are also depicted as valuing service and being empathic significantly less than media physicians. (p. 184)

The Kalisches (Ibid.) concluded that

the contribution of the nurse to health care as portrayed in the entertainment media has been distinctly underplayed, and conversely the role of the physician has been presented in an exaggerated, idealistic, and heroic light. (p.185)

The Kalisches' studies also reveal that media portrayals of work often confuse occupational domains. For example, they found that physicians are shown to provide "both outstanding medical care *and* nursing care" (Ibid., p. 189) with the result that "the public is led to believe that no special body of nursing knowledge and skill exists and that physicians can step in at any point in time and provide excellent nursing care" (p. 189). This exaggeration of the power of physicians is also evident in another of the Kalisches' studies which involved an analysis of the media blitz surrounding the birth of the Dionne Quintuplets (Kalisch and Kalisch, 1984). Here they found that in movies depicting the lives of these children the physician was portrayed to be "like God Himself, the perfectly loving father-figure, the perfectly wise counselor, the perfectly skilled miracle worker" (p. 249). In contrast, the nurses in these films

could scarcely hope to compete with the dazzling image of the saintly physician. . .they were the doctor's loving, trusted, competent helpmates, but they performed almost no duties requiring any expertise, nor did they demonstrate any real importance in health care. (p. 249)

According to the Kalisches, such imagery has had a negative long-term impact on the nursing profession because the public

inherited the ideal—the image of the courageous country doctor and the devoted, happily subservient nurse. This archetypal image has proven nearly indelible and presents a formidable obstacle to efforts to enhance the current image of the nurse. (p. 250)

Nursing stereotypes continue to prevail with the result that they are seldom acknowledged for their expertise whereas physicians "receive credit for virtually all positive health care outcomes—a discrepancy reinforced by the print and electronic media" (Kalisch and Kalisch, 1983b, p. 48). The Kalisches claim that through such misrepresentations of occupational roles in health care, the media harm efforts to recruit new people to nursing, negatively influence the allocation of revenue and research funding, and damage the self-image and confidence of nurses.

Images of Women

Relatively little attention in the Kalisches' analyses have been devoted to the issue of gender even though their data reveal many examples of the gendered nature of work roles in health care. Their findings indicate, for instance, that the media portrays nursing to be so straightforward and lacking in complexity that anyone with a nurturing disposition could do it quite easily. This is a theme which has, of course, been consistently identified in different types of analyses of the female professions. For example, Meade (1986) observed that on television, most nurses are not only depicted in either a maternal or romantic light, but are also shown to have "few intellectual abilities" (p. 25). (Librarians might take heart from this since while their image may be staid and boring, in contrast with the nurses they are also usually perceived to be bright or at least "bookish.")
According to Bem (1983),

> female behavior is interpreted to fit the stereotype of what women are like, and one important aspect of the female stereotype in American society is that females are incompetent except in certain highly stereotyped roles such as wife and mother. (p. 42)

Therefore, the media's use of caricatures about the female professions is simply a useful mechanism through which to promote a particular plot line involving women. In other words, that a woman might be a nurse or employed in any other occupation is merely incidental, instead, her major feature is that of being female (Gallagher, 1987).
Given this feature of media portrayals of women's work, it is probably not surprising that when women are occasionally depicted in more challenging work roles they are shown to be somewhat less than "feminine." For instance, in a study of the images of psychiatric nurses in films, Kalisch and Kalisch (1981) found that while these nurses had more power in their jobs and were consulted more often by physicians than is true of other types of cinema nurses, they were also portrayed as less physically attractive, more emotionally disturbed, and more abusive of their power. A related aspect of media portrayals of the female-intensive professions is that they tend to depict men, rather than women, in leadership positions. For example, Bourkoff and Wooldridge's (1986) examination of the portrayals of librarians in American newspapers revealed that male library

administrators tended to be featured; however, when reference was made to practicing librarians they were usually women.

Stereotyping of the Male Professions

The stereotyped images of the female-intensive occupations are quite different than those one might encounter in depictions of male fields, such as engineering. Engineers, too, rue their "lack of pay, lack of status and lack of recognition" (Lidgate, 1988, p. 251) and attribute these problems, in part, to their public image. However, although some have complained about problematic personal imagery, such as that of the engineer "as a (male) loner and a nerd" (Bell and Janowski, 1988, p. 133), a more serious image problem faced by engineers has to do with the public's lack of knowledge about this occupation. According to Bell and Janowski (Ibid.), media portrayals of engineering usually incorporate the notion that it is "bewilderingly technical;" however, they

> seldom project a clear picture of what an engineer is or does. . . in fact, out-side of the technical world, people don't distinguish between engineers and scientists. (p. 132)

So, while engineers may indeed be stereotyped as lonely men who are lacking in social skills, this image goes hand-in-hand with a presumption of brilliance. This makes for quite an interesting contrast between the occupational stereotypes of the male and female professions. Generally, the female fields are seen to require the "natural" talents of women but not much intellect, whereas the male professions require competence and great intellectual ability. Therefore, it is not surprising that the lack of self-esteem which is so pervasive in the female-intensive occupations is not evident in the literatures of engineering or other male disciplines, such as law. A survey of electrical engineers revealed, for example, that although they were concerned about what they saw to be a lack of social and finan-cial recognition of their field, many felt that "engineering had a greater impact on society than other professions" (Santo, 1988, p. 136). This is, of course, hardly a statement one associates with a lack of self-confidence.

PEERS' PERCEPTIONS OF THE FEMALE-INTENSIVE FIELDS

Within the female professions, concerns about image are not only reflected in studies of the popular media. Instead, suspecting that their colleagues accord them as little status as do members of the public, librarians and nurses often collect data about how members of their own and other fields perceive their occupations. One of the more famous examples of this in librarianship is Wilson's (1982) investigation of the occupational stereotypes to be found in documents written by librarians between 1921 and 1978 in which she observed that negative stereotypes of librarianship are maintained through "librarians writing about the stereotype, masters' students writing theses on the topic, various publications of library organizations, and various research studies exploring the attitudes and characteristics of librarians" (p. 68).[1]

Reaching outside the field, Divay, Ducas, and Michaud-Oystryk (1987) surveyed university faculty members about their perceptions of campus academic librarians who not only had faculty status but were included in the same bargaining unit. Their findings indicated that few members of the faculty saw librarians as real academics. Rather, they favored a view of the librarian as a professional employee who provides a service function to the university. And, while they valued such a service, the faculty members who responded to this survey certainly did not regard librarians as their academic peers. This view of academic librarians is not confined to faculty members. Students, too,

> generally confuse the functions and qualifications of library staff and perceive librarians as service oriented and as having less variety of duties than they actually have. (Hernon and Pastine, 1977, p. 135)

Using a method similar to that of Divay et al. (1987), Lippman and Ponton (1989) studied faculty members' perceptions of nurses in universities which offered baccalaureate nursing programs. They interpreted the results of their survey in a very positive light, concluding that "nursing faculty have earned a place on the university campus" (p. 27). However, their optimism may have been somewhat misplaced since fully one-third of the faculty members who responded did *not* agree that "nursing faculty are peers with other university faculty" (p. 27).

For members of nursing and library science faculties, the results of these types of studies must be less than satisfying. Although the findings indicate that the members of these faculties are seen to play a legitimate and valued role within their host institutions, the results also show that they are not really seen to be on a par with their other academic colleagues within the university. Rather, the other professors (whose occupation is,

---

[1] Curiously, however, Wilson (1982) devoted little of her analysis to addressing the reasons why these images have developed. Incredibly, one reviewer (Blake, 1983) who was critical of Wilson's failure to address this issue was herself roundly criticized for "advancing her own social concerns" (Stevens, 1988, p. 841).

by the way, one of the highest in prestige of the all traditionally male professions) perceive faculty members in the "women's departments" to be working in other than an academic role, that is, in the less prestigious capacities of service-provider and teacher.

RECRUITMENT TO THE PROFESSION

As noted earlier, many members of the female-intensive fields are of the opinion that negative stereotypes about their occupations inhibit recruitment. In social work, for example, Euster (1980) stressed the need to improve the image of the field in order to

> attract qualified young people to the profession...indeed, the profession must reshape its image so that the community views social workers as knowledgeable, well trained, research orientated, and visibly concerned with solving community problems. (p. 283)

Imagery has also been an issue in nurse recruitment. Salvage (1983) complained that a British recruitment ad for nurses which declared that the best nurses have the essential qualifications *before* they go to school "was perhaps the worst example of publicity which did not emphasise the skills and challenges of the job, but implied that all you needed to be a nurse was innate niceness" (p. 8). She also pointed out, however, that the recruiting literature is gradually improving to the extent that it is beginning to market nursing "as a desirable career for the intelligent, the motivated and the highly qualified applicant" (p. 8).

In librarianship, too, recruitment to the field has been hampered by image problems. In fact, British high school career counsellors reportedly feel that the unfortunate public image of librarians and information workers is a major problem facing the profession which "acts as a barrier to the entry of the right kind of people into the profession, and to career advancement once employed" (Slater, 1987, p. 341). To overcome this barrier, counsellors have urged members of the field "to mount a campaign to dispel the stereotype and to promote a more positive modern image" (p. 341).

Improving the Quality of Recruits

Recruitment involves not just attracting greater numbers of people to the female-intensive fields, but bringing in "better" people, thereby enhancing the status of these professions. This theme is echoed through the women's fields. In home economics, Whatley (1974) described the need for greater rigor in recruitment, while in nursing Hammer and Tufts (1985) observed that if the profession "hopes to propagate and nurture a positive image, it should start with the type of student it admits" (p. 281). Through these arguments runs a thread of the same type of inward-looking, self-blame that was described in the previous chapter. Indeed, according to Hammer and Tufts (Ibid.), nurses should note that

> low self-esteem and poor self-image do not seem to be a problem among practising physicians. Perhaps nursing should imitate medicine's approach, and consciously practice respect for and belief in the capabilities of students. (p. 283)

Their comment implies that nurses do not, in fact, respect one another or their students and that the lack of self-esteem within the profession is the result of the flaws of its members rather than stereotyping that arises from sources external to the field.

This type of thinking is also evident in library literature in which there have been numerous calls to weed out undesirables from the field. Concomitant with demands for better selection processes is research directed at identifying the so-called "librarian personality." For a time (especially during the 1960s and 1970s), there was a steady stream of articles and books published in which were described the results of various personality tests that had been given to librarians. The goal of this type of research was to determine whether librarians, as a group, were different from the members of other occupations. The assumption underlying this research seems to be that if certain characteristics such as timidity or prudishness did indeed distinguish librarians from others, they might provide an explanation for the low status of the field. Furthermore, in the event that such characteristics could be readily detected, personality tests might then be used during recruiting to select out those who showed evidence of such unfortunate tendencies and prevent them from entering the field, thereby enhancing the profession.

Fortunately, one sees less and less of this type of research in today's library literature because, of course, the ethical issues it raises are extremely problematic. First of all, personality tests themselves are controversial, often being of questionable reliability and validity (see, for example, Newmeyer, 1976). Second, the use of personality tests to weed out prospective candidates from educational programs raises various legal questions, particularly as it is becoming increasingly difficult to justify selection decisions on any grounds other than past academic performance. Finally, it may be that such an approach would favor the increased selection of men over women into the field since it is "femininity," in the view of some, that is responsible for the low status of the female professions (see, for example, Garrison, 1979, in librarianship and Sadler, 1984, in nursing).[2]

The notion of selection by gender is not as farfetched as it might seem. Both Hildenbrand (1985) and Bernard (1983) have commented on the very deliberate strategy of importing men into some of the women's professions in order to increase their status. Furthermore, some authors have hinted at the possible link between high female enrollment levels and poor academic quality of students (although usually in a somewhat indirect fashion). For example, in a comment on the declining enrollment in undergraduate and graduate social work programs in the United States, Siporin (1984) noted that

> the quality of students accepted in these programs has declined sharply, and the proportion of women students has increased to 78 percent. (p. 238)

SELF-MARKETING

Recruitment tactics are only one of many strategies that have been suggested for increasing the status of the female fields. In addition to bringing in better people and keeping undesirables out, various methods have been proposed for improving those who are already in the field, however they were selected. As noted in Chapter 4, self-improvement is a common theme wherein nurses, librarians, and so on are urged to project themselves in a more positive light. One might think of this as a sort of personal marketing strategy. For instance, the director of the American Library Association's public relations office offered various tips to librarians who want to enhance their images including advice to

> dress more stylishly. Let's show the world that we are professional men and women who are also attractive, smart and powerful. Dress for success. (Wallace, 1989, p. 25)

Similarly, in a workshop called "What's your I.Q." (the term I.Q. was used to refer to the participants' "Image Quotient"), librarians were encouraged to promote themselves and to "dress distinctively, and build personal power, be assertive, decisive, self-reliant, dynamic and charis-

---

[2] Of course, it should be noted that the very notion of "femininity" as opposed to "masculinity" is itself a matter of some debate among psychologists. For example, it has been argued that the characteristics traditionally associated with male and female social roles are, in fact, independent of one another, that is, these characteristics are not necessarily mutually exclusive. In other words, individuals who possess "feminine" characteristics, such as nurturance, may also exhibit "masculine" characteristics, such as competitiveness.

matic" (Rasmussen, 1988, p. 12). Using nearly the same language, Bush
and Kjervik (1979) urged nurses "to present themselves in an assertive
manner as professionals who are convinced of their self-worth" (p. 697),
while Porter, Porter, and Lower (1989) encouraged them to portray a
positive image in dress, speech, and action; articulate the role of nursing
in providing comprehensive health care; and practice with compassion,
knowledge, commitment, and competence.

Socialization into image consciousness starts from the moment students
enter the women's professions. In fact, in one article written for student
nurses it was noted that "the best place to start changing nursing's image
. . . is within yourself" ("How can I change the image of nursing?," 1988,
p. 79). Again, such suggestions are very much in keeping with the feminization hypothesis. The tendency to see the problems facing these fields as
an indicator of some kind of internal deficiency is vividly illustrated by
Sapp's (1987) observation that librarians must simply do better in carrying
out their jobs because "contrived efforts to globally improve our image
attack the symptom but ignore the *disease*" (Ibid., p. 136; emphasis mine).
The important thing to remember, of course, is that there is no evidence
of this disease. In other words, it is not at all clear that librarians, nurses,
and others in the female-intensive occupations do *not* present themselves
assertively, dress appropriately, and behave in a self-reliant and competent manner to at least the same degree as those who are members of other
more admired occupational groups.

MARKETING THE FEMALE PROFESSIONS

An alternative to enhancing the image of the female-intensive professions
by pressuring members to improve themselves is to market these aspiring
occupations by manipulating their media images. "Image management"
campaigns involve the development of an organized response to media
stereotyping as well as "fostering an improved image" (Kalisch and Kalisch,
1983a, p. 480). While this seems simple enough on the surface, in order to
undertake such a campaign, members of these professions must agree on
the type of image they wish to see projected about their occupation. Reaching such an agreement is not always easy. For example, when a group of
nurses organized to protest a 1981 *Playboy* decision to do a feature on
nurses, the members of the group were unable at first to achieve any consensus on nursing's role in the health care system (Evans, Fitzpatrick, and
Howard-Ruben, 1983).

Despite such difficulties, however, the idea of promoting occupations
through public relations campaigns is nothing new. In the 1970s, Whatley
(1974) recommended that home economists use public relations personnel

to promote the social relevance of home economics. Her recommendation, however, was echoed over a decade later by Inana (1984) who, noting that home economists have a "serious public relations problem," urged them to "make greater efforts to alert parents, local school personnel, and other policy makers that our programs are basic and do support academic subjects" (p. 170).

One method for achieving this public awareness is for professional associations to offer television networks advice about occupational roles. According to Abbott (1981), the public is most admiring of "effective contact with the disorderly" (p. 830) and while "this power over disorder is most obvious in medicine, psychiatry, law, and the clergy, in fact all the professions attempt to tame disorder or to create new order" (p. 830). Therefore, Abbott (Ibid.) suggested that one way to build an occupation's prestige is to mount systematic public relations campaigns that are designed to persuade the public that a particular professional group is effective in dealing with what he called "public charismatic disorder" (p. 832).

Recognizing this, along with the important public relations possibilities in television, the American Medical Association (A.M.A.) founded the Physicians Advisory Committee to Television, Radio and Motion Pictures in 1955. Through this mechanism, the A.M.A. has been able to bring to the public's attention the physician's skills in taming disease and bringing calm and order to distressing situations. Similarly, albeit with somewhat less success, the National Association of Social Workers was involved as early as the 1960s in a production of the television series "East-side/west-side" in an attempt to convey an accurate and sympathetic image of social work (Andrews, 1987).

Librarians have yet to be faced with the need to advise producers of a dramatic television series about library work. However, some opportunities for influencing the popular media do exist. In their study of the print media's portrayal of librarianship, Bourkoff and Wooldridge (1986) found that library-related stories are seldom reported on the front pages of newspapers (instead, they are normally located in the arts and culture section) and that

> while the stereotypical library roles are still being presented by the press, there is sufficient coverage to the contrary to suggest that libraries are succeeding in presenting librarians as vital, active, and progressive. (p. 62)

Given that the press does seem somewhat favorably disposed toward libraries, Bourkoff and Wooldridge urged librarians to take a more proactive stance vis-à-vis the media, that is, to "grasp the initiative" and take "responsibility for what reaches their public through newspapers and other media" (Ibid.).

Using the Language of Power

Beyond initiating contact with the media, Kalisch and Kalisch (1983a) recommended an even more manipulative strategy of image management. They encouraged nurses to "fabricate" a powerful image for themselves through the media, arguing that

> to the extent that the mass media serve an agenda-setting function, we are calling for their conscious employment in effecting a transformation of the image of the nurse which emphasizes equality, commitment to career, and renunciation of nursing as a physician-dominated occupation demanding an impossible degree of obedience. Substitution of androgyny for traditional rigid female imagery in media nurse representations would effectively provide alternative role models that would begin to open nursing up as a strong career option for both sexes. (p. 19)

Others in the female-intensive fields have also called on their colleagues to create for themselves an image of power. For instance, because social workers tend to work in organizations dominated by more powerful professional groups, Jansson and Simmons (1986) suggested that they devise an image that would increase their visibility and influence with these groups. They suggested that social workers should identify the criteria valued by these other professions and market an image of social work that is consistent with these criteria. Librarians have also been encouraged to "get out and market their services" (Slater, 1987, p. 336). In fact, an editorial in the *Journal of Academic Librarianship* ("Power of Images," 1988), urged librarians to build a "vital, authoritative image" based on their "vast repertoire of problem-solving skills" (p. 139). Noting that the negative image of librarians adversely affects the standing of the profession, Major Owens, a former librarian and member of the United States House of Representatives, suggested that practitioners "possess constructive arrogance when establishing their authority over matters relative to library and information services" ("Image: How They're Seeing Us," (1986, p. 502).

Although librarians have been somewhat tardy in adopting an aggressive public relations stance (relative to their counterparts in other female-intensive fields), they are beginning to employ increasingly sophisticated responses to the image problem. Library literature contains many reports about image conferences and groups of librarians who are organizing to combat their image problems by hiring publicists and, even in some cases, contracting with political lobbyists to present their point of view to legislators. One of these lobbyists, hired by librarians from the University of Washington, advised that librarians should decide on the image they want to project and band together to achieve it. This lobbyist also noted that the fragmentation of librarians into many organizations, each with its own agenda, is confusing to legislators who "are not hostile to librarians, but they are often ignorant of what librarians do" (Richards and Elliot, 1988, p. 424).

Public Relations Campaigns

Under the auspices of the professional associations in nursing and librarianship, several major public education campaigns have been undertaken over the past decade. For instance, in 1981 the U.S. National League for Nursing established a task force on nursing's public image. In 1982, the American Academy of Nursing devoted its annual meeting to "Image-making in nursing." Following close behind their American counterparts, British nurses set up the Public Image of Nursing Campaign or "PINC" in 1983. In some jurisdictions, these publicity campaigns are run on an ongoing basis. For instance, the Ontario Nurses Association sponsors an annual "Nurses' Week" in order to raise the profile of nursing in the community.

Recently, some similar image marketing intiatives have been organized in librarianship. However, one of the key differences between the approaches taken by nurses and librarians is that whereas the promotional strategies used by nurses focus on the nursing profession itself, the library associations tend to focus their campaigns on libraries rather than librarians. For example, the American Library Association sponsors "National *Library* Week." This emphasis has not gone unchallenged by members of the profession. Veaner (1985), for instance, argued that librarians should be promoted just as much as library collections, noting that the Association of College and Research Libraries did just that in 1982 by highlighting the role of academic librarians in bibliographic instruction to several different professional associations including the American Council of Learned Societies. Another outspoken critic of the American Library Association's policy of marketing that "sells libraries but doesn't feature or even mention librarians" concluded that "the public assumes, out of an ignorance we have never corrected, that any one who works in a library is a librarian" (White, 1986, p. 58). Apparently these pressures have begun to have an effect. In 1989, the A.L.A. altered the focus of its marketing campaign to

> promote awareness of the librarian as a professional, to make people think 'information' and 'librarian' the same way they think 'doctor' when they're sick or 'lawyer' when they have legal problems. . . and to present librarianship as an attractive career opportunity. (Wallace, 1989, p. 24)

THE IMPACT OF IMAGE PROMOTION

The considerable investment made by the professional associations in promoting a new image for the female-intensive occupations begs the question as to whether or not these campaigns have been at all effective. At present, there is little direct evidence available about the impact of marketing occupational images. However, indirect indices suggest that these efforts have effected little significant change in the status of the female fields. In nursing, for instance, the shortage of qualified nurses is so severe that there is increasing pressure throughout the health care system to locate and, in some cases, lure nurses away from their present jobs. Despite this very strong seller's market, the number of students enrolling in nursing programs has declined. And, while the visibility of nursing may be on the rise as a result of several serious job actions taken by nurses over the past few years, it has not translated into tremendous salary gains (at least not in comparison with the earnings of physicians). Furthermore, the increased visibility of the nursing profession has also done little to stem the numbers of experienced nurses who are no longer willing to work in hospital settings or who are leaving the profession entirely in order to pursue other careers. In social work, too, a serious crisis is evident in many social service agencies as many of the most experienced workers leave salaried positions in favor of more lucrative private practices (Blumenstein, 1988).

Although librarians tend to be less unhappy about their working conditions than do their counterparts in nursing and social work, a recent editorial in *American Libraries* suggested that salary level is still very much a sore point. Attributing the salary problem to an oversupply of librarians, Kniffel (1990) suggested that "the price of a librarian, like the price of caviar, would go up if the shelves weren't stocked to overflowing" (p. 476) and recommended that the A.L.A. should *not* attempt to avert a national shortage of librarians. Despite Kniffel's optimism about the regulating powers of the market, however, the example of nursing suggests that the supply-and-demand theory of wage control does not necessarily apply in the female-intensive professions. In other words, reducing the availability of trained nurses, social workers, and librarians is no guarantee of greater remuneration. If anything, the history of these occupations suggests that in the case of shortages, employers simply fill the empty slots with less qualified, lower paid workers on the assumption that, as noted earlier, women's work requires little in the way of special skill.

ALTERNATIVES TO MARKETING

The portrayals of nursing, social work, and librarianship in the popular media did not alter substantially during the last decade despite the public education campaigns and various attempts to influence the media. So, if marketing does not work and the images have not changed, what is left to do about occupational stereotyping and lack of prestige in the female-intensive professions?

Most members of the women's fields are ready to acknowledge that occupational image, that is, the public's perceptions of these occupations, is very much connected to low status and poor pay associated with this type of work. However, despite this agreement, the solutions that are recommended for overcoming the image problem remain as varied as ever. Some continue to take the view that public perceptions will change as the members of these occupations improve themselves. Muff (1988), for example, claimed that

> real-life encounters with flesh-and-blood nurses will do more to mitigate the damage of media stereotypes than our most vociferous protests. I don't mean to imply that television Handmaidens and Battle Axes will vanish if ignored. They won't. . . . Yet, as nurses gain in self-awareness and confidence, the public image will come to reflect these changes. (p. 48)

Using virtually the same argument, Kelly (1989) claimed that "the best image making is reality" (p. 17). Furthermore, she went on to suggest that

> if enough real nurses practice professionally with competence and caring, if they create, direct and/or practice in innovative settings that provided needed care to patients, if they are risk-takers not afraid to develop or assume 'different' roles in health care, if with research they find answers to better patient care, if they look beyond the crisis-centered here and now to anticipate and search out ways to meet the public's health care needs, if they simply demonstrate the existing diversity of nursing, there will be likeminded men and women who will see nursing as a worthwhile career opportunity. (p. 17)

One sees in such arguments the continued belief that change in the status of the female fields depends on the individual efforts of people who are employed in these occupations. In other words, it is assumed that hard work and competent service will, eventually, be rewarded. This further assumes, of course, that nurses, librarians, and others in the women's professions have not provided competent service or worked hard in the past, a rather more difficult supposition to sell, especially to older practitioners.

Recognizing the problems with these arguments, some members of the female fields, impatient with their inability to change the status/pay configuration, have chosen to become politically active in order to achieve their goals. For instance, as early as the 1970s, Kalisch and Kalisch (1976) recommended that nurses get involved in politics in order to change the health care environment. According to them, politically speaking, the model nurse is not the quiet, submissive, hardwork-ing individual who makes the best of every situation, but the cold, calculat-ing professional who uses all available resources to advance the health care world around her. (p. 33)

The need for such an approach was pointed out by Brown (1975) who noted that

organized nursing has far less power in the health service industry than one would expect of an occupation of so many workers and so key to the industry. The American Nursing Association (ANA) and the National League for Nurs-ing (NLN) are generally ignored by the health service industry elite and its outside supporters on questions of public policy with respect to health care. (p. 176)

Unfortunately, despite the fact that many nurses have heeded this advice and become increasingly vocal and more politicized as a result, they have yet to achieve a substantial change in their salaries, status, or influence within the health care system.

COMING TO TERMS WITH THE STEREOTYPING OF WOMEN

The failure of nursing to have achieved its goals despite years of struggle suggests that it may be time for the members of the female-intensive fields to rethink the barriers they face. It may be especially useful to rethink exactly what is being portrayed through the imagery associated with their occupations, particularly with respect to sex-role stereotyping. As Bem (1983) suggested, it is probably not so much the stereotype of the work undertaken in these fields that is at the root of the problems they face, but rather the fact that the stereotype is of women. In nursing, for example, the stereotypes of nurses

are not merely a travesty of what real nurses are and what they do. They are closely related to the male-defined images of women which we find wherever we look. Images of nursing always fall within that framework and gain their currency from it—including the male nurse stereotype, the limp-wristed gay, which is a product of the same oppressive system and an equally crude distor-tion of reality. (Salvage, 1983, p. 13) [3]

---

[3] Similar homophobic stereotypes about men in a women's profession also appear from time to time in library literature.

Creating a Feminist Profession

Recognizing that it is the perception of women that is really at issue for the female-intensive professions, some members of these fields have argued that working for the advancement of women is the strategy most likely to produce a positive change in their occupations. For example, Weibel (1976) called for the transition of librarianship from a "feminized" profession to a "feminist" one, that is, to a profession that operates "on a feminist value system wherein traditional roles based on sex and power are no longer extant" (p. 264). Although Weibel's ideas have been slow to be accepted, some leadership in this direction has been in evidence recently within the library associations. For instance, the director of the A.L.A.'s public information office has acknowledged that systemic factors outside the field itself have determined the status of librarianship. She noted the image of the field "reflects complex social and cultural forces that have shortchanged traditionally 'female' professions—both in dollars and respect" (Wallace, 1989, p. 24).

Although Weibel's challenge has yet to receive widespread acceptance within the library field, it has been adopted, to some extent, by those in the nursing profession. Baumgart (1980) noted, for instance, that

> if nursing is to keep up the pressure to have its interests better represented, it is important for nurses, individually and collectively, to be aware of some of the ways in which sexism contributed to their political inexperience and lack of political influence. (p. 6)

Similarly, Salvage (1983) observed that many of the problems faced by nurses

> derive from the traditional link between nursing and women's work, and the traditional attitudes about women which from babyhood undermine our confidence in ourselves and often prevent us from reaching our full potential. (p. 182)

Making a similar connection, the president-elect of the Registered Nurses Association of Ontario observed that

> it will be difficult for nurses to obtain first-class status in health care while society treats most women as second-class citizens.... The solution lies in becoming aware of where power lies within the system and how nurses have been socialized to accept and maintain it. (Thomas, 1990, p. 14)

Structural barriers face all women in the workplace and, as long as they exist, the female-intensive professions will be unable to attain the level of status and remuneration accorded to comparable male professions. Thus, no matter how hard the members of the women's fields try to improve the quality of their work and set for themselves the task of leaping over ever-higher hurdles of credentialism, specialization, and research, they will not achieve the recognition to which they aspire. Furthermore, regardless of how sophisticated and expensive their image campaigns are, they will not overcome negative stereotyping until they recognize that it is the image of women and the value of women's endeavor, not the image of particular occupations such as nursing or librarianship, that is responsible for their status in the workforce. Thus, although in the following comment Baumgart (1980) was referring particularly to nursing, her remarks are relevant to all those who work in the female professions:

> It would be naive and politically hazardous to tackle the problem of sex-role stereotyping simply by attempting to bolster the persuasive powers of nurses or by cultivating a new public image of nursing. These strategies fiddle with effects rather than coming to grip with causes and so rationalize and maintain the existing power structure. (p. 13)

It seems, then, that the best response to the image problem in the female-intensive fields may be for the members of these occupations to join together with others in the women's movement, in other words, to recognize that theirs is a shared problem—one that goes beyond occupational boundaries and which reflects instead the gendered nature of the workplace.[4]

---

[4] Although not joining together on the basis of this feminist theme, there is some recognition that a united effort is necessary in order to enhance the image of librarianship. In 1989, the president of the Special Libraries Associations started the Inter Association Task Force on the Enhancement of the Image of the Librarian/Information Professional. The task force includes representatives from several associations including the American Library Association, the American Society for Information Science, the American School Library Association, and the Canadian Library Association.

CHAPTER 6

Unions and Associations: Who Speaks for the Workers?

As noted many times in the previous chapters, much of the impetus for professionalization in the female-intensive occupations is rooted in dissatisfaction over salary levels. However, despite widespread agreement that pressure for better remuneration is needed, not everyone agrees on the mechanisms that should generate this pressure. In some of these fields the professional associations have taken on the job of pursuing higher wages for their members, while in others the associations have steered clear of this responsibility, leaving it instead to the unions.

UNIONISM VERSUS PROFESSIONALISM

According to Winter (1988), the role of the professional associations in occupational regulation is to develop

> standards for routine work, definitions of professionalism, broad statements of policy affecting the delivery of services, clarifications of the basic attitudes and values underlying the work, and support for research and scholarship to improve professional practice. (p. 58)

In North America, associations of social workers, teachers, nurses, and librarians perform all these functions; however, they tend to operate somewhat differently in each field. For instance, teachers and nurses have been inclined "to improve their salaries, working conditions, and social status through stronger and more powerful unions" (Humphreys and Dinerman, 1984, p. 210) and many of their associations operate in a manner similar to that of unions. Indeed, some are directly involved in collective bargaining on behalf of their membership.

Social workers and librarians, on the other hand, have tended instead to pursue the route of professionalization rather than unionism in order to achieve their occupational goals and, as a result, their associations typically do not participate in activities that are directly concerned with the conditions of employment. For example, the National Social Work Association (a large, umbrella association for social workers in the United States), like its counterpart, the American Library Association, has not been actively involved in collective bargaining.[1] In fact, Humphreys and Dinerman (1984) observed that American social workers have, for the most part,

> failed to join or form unions and avoid using unions to advance their claims. Current data on the extent of union membership among social workers are not available; there are not even reliable estimates. It is believed that union membership, particularly among MSWs, is small and nowhere near the levels found among nurses and teachers. (p. 210)

In librarianship, the ideology of professionalism, embodied in the library associations, has come under periodic attack, leading Wilson (1981) to observe that "in one form or another, the American Library Association has to deal with all the manifestations of the attack on professionalism" (p. 285). Estabrook (1981a), for example, claimed that it is this ideology

> which prevents librarians from organizing into unions, obscures the fundamental difference between labor and management within library organizations, and creates tension and conflict between librarians and their clients.... As an occupational group which strives to achieve the status of professionalism, librarians are severely threatened by activities which, in effect, ally them with blue-collar workers. (p. 125)

Making a similar point, Nelson (1980) noted that

> if money were the primary objective of the quest for professionalism, then we would have expected organizations like unions, the major aim of which is improving the earnings of their members, to have had a greater impact on relatively low-paying occupations like librarianship. Yet unions have been resisted —branded as 'unprofessional.' The underlying objection is that unions are organizations of the wrong class of society. (p. 2031)

---

[1] In contrast with their American counterparts, Canadian social workers have been involved for many years in strong social work unions (Humphreys and Dinerman, 1984).

McDermott (1984), too, complained that if librarians "continue to look to the 'true' professions as our ideal model, if we continue to argue that we are undervalued and unappreciated as 'professionals,' it will be to our own economic disadvantage" (p. 18). She recommended instead that librarians "join labor organizations and feminist groups in pursuing pay equity or comparable worth approaches" (p. 21). She went on to point out, with not a little sarcasm, that

> if the point is to cling to some ideal, but fuzzy concept of what constitutes 'professional' behavior, a concept which would exclude lawsuits and collective bargaining, let's just wait until the situation gets even worse. That way no one could ever accuse us of being in it for the money, like lawyers and doctors. (p. 21)

Professionalism has also been criticized for contributing to tension between the members of the female fields. As noted in earlier chapters, class distinctions are inherent in the professional model of occupational development and have led to considerable tension. Estabrook (1981a) commented on this problem in librarianship, noting that

> we suffer so under our own inadequate professional salaries that we fight with those of lesser status for the low wages we are offered. Instead of collective action against an inequitable social system, we squabble to affirm our own superiority by obeisance to the philosophy of professionalism. (p. 126)

Noting a similar lack of willingness to take collective action in order to improve working conditions in nursing, Hammond (1990) observed that if nurses would just accept that theirs is a semi-profession rather than a "real" profession, nursing leaders would work harder at unionizing.[2]

The controversy over whether or not library workers should unionize has been rumbling since the early part of this century. According to Garrison (1979), whether they represented lower grade library assistants or senior staff members, the early library unionists

> demanded not only better salaries and working conditions but also an end to sexual discrimination in hiring and promotion. Antiunionists charged that union members were materialistic and self-serving—were, in fact, unfeminine. (p. 229)

Lingering anxieties about the femininity of women who demand wage increases are still evident in much of North American society. One need only

---

[2] Hammond (1990) was also of the opinion that by moving away from an emphasis on professionalism, nursing leaders would be more likely to press for competency-based college training rather than university education for all nurses.

look at the public's reactions to striking nurses to see that caring functions are expected to transcend financial concerns. Nurses (and public school teachers) who withdraw their services in strikes are often vilified and cast, at the very least, as "strident," if not "mercenary."

Another concern sometimes voiced about the impact of unions in librarianship is over the potential discord they might create within the bureaucratic hierarchy that is typical of library organizations. According to Schlachter (1976),

> if harmony and loyalty between managers and professional staff are essential elements in professionalism, then any force which appears disruptive would be viewed as disloyal and therefore unprofessional. Frequently, unions are viewed as instruments which create a 'damaging adversary relation with management' by fostering conflict and hostility between staff professionals and administration. As a result, unions have often been considered quite unnecessary and unprofessional. (p. 458)

Such a view was expressed, for example, by Meyer (1980), who argued against unions for academic librarians. He claimed that a union

> locks the professional into a situation where he is forced to follow the majority. When the union is university-wide, librarians represent a minority which suffers significant loss of autonomy. Each librarian will not simply be judged by 'peers' but will be directed by them. In addition, the collective bargaining situation sets up an adversary relationship which leads to the elimination of middle management. This results in a loss of status particularly for department heads. (p. 280)[3]

In spite of such fears, however, many public library workers in large urban centers belong to unions, school librarians are often absorbed into teachers' unions, and many academic librarians are members of faculty unions, although, as will be discussed in more detail later, many of these academic librarians have been losing their collective bargaining rights as many of the faculty unions in the United States have been decertified over the past decade.

As Schlacter (1973) explained,

> the same factors which created a favorable climate for collective bargaining among nurses and teachers—employment concentration, economic imbalance, limited job advancement, and job insecurity—are increasingly characteristic of the field of librarianship. (p. 458)

---

[3] Meyer (1980) did not reserve his criticism for unions alone. He was equally critical of the faculty model for academic librarians because it "attempts to elevate one segment of the profession above the rest . . . and submits the profession to evaluation by criteria ill suited to the mission of librarianship" (p. 278).

Thus, for librarians, as for many others in the female-intensive fields, unionism offers an attractive alternative to professionalism as a means for achieving such goals as improved salaries as well as greater status and power vis-à-vis other occupational groups. Part of the attraction of unions is due to the subordinate status of the members of these fields. According to Larson (1977),

> the structural predisposition toward collective bargaining power will be greater wherever an aspiring profession is subordinate to a hierarchy of authority, which itself includes categories with 'superior' claims of expertise. The case of hospital nurses and hospital technicians appear to warrant the hypothesis: since no amount of externally sanctioned expertise can compensate for the subordination of auxiliary medical professions to the physician, unionization remains a choice at least as effective as further professionalization. (p. 185)

PROFESSIONAL ASSOCIATIONS
AND COLLECTIVE BARGAINING

Frustration with the lack of progress made by the library associations in achieving better conditions for their members resulted in library workers' willingness to unionize. Given this willingness, one might reasonably ask why these associations have not assumed greater leadership by taking on the role of collective bargaining agents for library workers by assuming a quasi-union status.

In coming to terms with the increase in union membership on the part of library workers, groups, such as the American Library Association, have attempted to become somewhat more employee-centered than in the past. Explaining how the shift to greater employee-centeredness occurs in the professions, Schlacter (1973) noted that

> many professionals who have been willing to accept the concept of collective bargaining have been unwilling to go beyond the confines of their professional association to accomplish it. Some fields, therefore, have developed ...a 'quasi union,' a professional society which, while maintaining its original professional base, adopts an employee orientation. Historically, this metamorphosis has occurred when unions began to conduct successful membership drives. In order to preserve hegemony, professional associations have attempted to make unionism unnecessary by behaving like a union in order to meet the interests and needs of their membership. (p. 186)

However, this metamorphosis has not taken place in librarianship and, as will be seen, the associations' policies reflect a considerable ambivalence vis-à-vis their role with respect to workers and management.

One of the significant impediments which prevented the library associations from making a successful shift to this quasi-union status and their failure to come to terms with employee-centered issues in the field is their peculiar membership structure. As noted earlier, the associations in social work and librarianship share some similarities. However, there is a fundamental difference in the way in which they are organized. In librarianship, unlike in social work (or, for that matter, in teaching or nursing), one is apt to find *library* rather than *librarian* associations. Thus, membership in the American Library Association, for example, is open to

> any person, library, or other organization interested in library service and librarianship...upon payment of the dues provided for in the Bylaws. (American Library Association, 1989, p. 210)

Similar membership structures are also found in the Canadian Library Association as well as in state and provincial associations, such as the Ontario Library Association. So, while only trained and qualified social workers are eligible to join the National Association of Social Workers, anyone can become a member of the American Library Association simply by paying a fee.

There have been attempts to depart from this model but they have not been particularly successful. The National Librarians Association, for instance, started in 1975 in response to the lack of status and low salaries in the profession, and because of the A.L.A.'s weak representation of librarians' concerns. However, its membership has never been great; from a high of 578 members in 1979, by 1987 it had dropped off to fewer than 300. Despite its failure to attract a significant membership, this group represents an interesting departure from others in the profession. Unlike associations such as the A.L.A., the N.L.A.'s mandate is explicit in its promotion of the profession of librarianship and in restricting its membership to those who hold a graduate degree in library science or who are enrolled in such a program (with exceptions granted only "to applicants who present evidence of outstanding contributions to the profession," National Librarians Association: Constitution, 1989, p. 5).

The other exceptions to the pattern of library rather than librarian associations are in other countries where one finds groups such as the Polish Librarians Association and the Norwegian Research Librarians Association. In many of these special interest groups within U.S. librarianship, however, such as the Asian/Pacific American Librarians Association (A.P.A.L.A.), the names may suggest an association that is focused on librarians' interests, but when one examines the membership requirements of these groups they are often comparable to that of the A.L.A. For instance, as is typical of associations of this type, membership in the

A.P.A.L.A. is open not only to librarians and information specialists of Asian/Pacific descent, but to libraries and other organizations as well as to anyone who subscribes to the purpose of the association. In other words, its membership is essentially open.

Perhaps more interesting in this regard are the library trustees and library technicians, both of whom have their own associations. Oddly enough, then, it is only the librarians who fail to have significant national associations in North America, relying instead on the A.L.A. and C.L.A. to represent their interests.

According to Reeves (1980), the open membership policy of the library associations and the "presence of 'nonprofessional' members, as well as the attention given to objectives that do not directly further the interests of librarians, has caused some commentators to despair" (p. 4). For example, Boissonnas (1972) observed that

> as long as ALA authorizes the employers of its members to belong, it will not be a librarians' organization. The American Medical Association is a doctors' organization, not one of the hospitals or medical schools, and the American Bar Association is an organization for lawyers, not law firms, courts, or law schools. (p. 978)

True to their names, the library associations tend to be library-centered rather than employee-centered with respect to such issues as salary and working conditions, leading Gwinnup (1974) to complain that the associations have

> been preoccupied with the repressive ideal of 'library service,' to the detriment of the profession and ultimately the public. Their love has been for libraries, not librarians. (p. 484)

Of course, not everyone agrees that the library associations should, in fact, be employee-centered. Todd (1985) argued, for instance, that by not taking an employee-centered stance associations, such as the A.L.A., have wisely avoided the various legal complications which have been encountered by other professional associations that organized themselves as quasi-unions. In fact, given the present membership configuration of the library associations, they would very likely be prevented from assuming a collective bargaining role on behalf of library employees. In order to fully understand this problem, it is instructive to consider some of the problems which have beset nursing associations in the United States.

As noted in earlier chapters, when nursing education moved out of the hospitals into academe, it resulted in higher status for nursing educators but not for the rank and file members of the nursing profession. Attempts to limit the R.N. designation to baccalaureate-trained nurses have not only been unsuccessful, but have generated a great deal of acrimony between nurses with different educational backgrounds for, as Dolan (1980) explained,

> professions are divided into elites and non-elites. The benefits of professional status are not apportioned equally among the classes within the profession. The quest for professional legal status by leaders of a vocation is also a quest for legal authority over the vocation's members by those leaders. (p. 44)

As a result of nursing's tiered class system, many non-baccalaureate trained nurses believe that they are "ignored or looked down upon by nursing's leaders and the baccalaureate-educated" (p. 44) and that the associations do not represent their interests. Their suspicions about the associations are not particularly surprising since they "tend to attract nurses more closely identified with the pursuit of professional stature: Nursing supervisors, educators and other elite categories" (p. 28).

That the particular membership mix in the nursing associations has had an effect on policy development seems undeniable. In fact, Dolan (Ibid.) concluded that

> nursing supervisors and educators are committed to wresting control of supervising nurses from hospital administrators and doctors. However, the nursing literature supports the conclusion that the reason for doing this is to transfer that power to nursing leaders—nursing theoreticians' euphemism for nursing bosses—not to dismantle the authoritarian hierarchy. As one nurse put it, nursing leaders do not call 'into question' the power and privilege at the apex of the medical hierarchy, but instead ask 'to be part of it.' (p. 29)

Although the nursing associations represent an enormous constituency (consider, for example, that registered nurses constitute the single largest profession in Canada), they exert relatively little control in health care as a whole and they are much less powerful than associations of lawyers or physicians. Their inability to wrest any meaningful level of control away from the health care elite means that the nursing associations have not been successful in negotiating the salaries or working conditions to which their members aspire. As a result, nurses have become increasingly interested in unionization. According to Dolan (Ibid.),

> hospitals have been notoriously bad payers for decades and have been adherents to one of the most highly stratified organizational structures outside the military. Relief for those at the bottom of the pyramid was indicated, and unionization continued to grow. This was no surprise, but many observers of the health care scene were taken aback by the rush to collective bargaining by the industry's professional employees. (p. 25)

The nursing associations have assumed the role of collective bargaining agents for their members; however, in so doing they encountered a serious problem. Because the membership in associations, such as the A.N.A., is top-heavy with better-educated nurses, many of whom work at the supervisory level, the associations have run afoul of U.S. labor legislation which prohibits "sweetheart unions," that is, unions organized by supervisors. The problem with such arrangements is obvious. As Dolan (Ibid.) observed,

> it is illogical to assume that a group dominated by supervisors could be expected to vigorously pursue the interests of rank-and-file members when, in all likelihood, a substantial number of the latter's complaints are aimed at those who supervise them. (p. 35)

Because of this potential for conflict of interest which is built into their membership structures, several legal decisions in U.S. courts will interfere with the nursing associations' ability to serve as collective bargaining agents for nurses. According to Dolan (Ibid.), these decisions

> brought out into the open the smouldering controversy over whether professional unity can be achieved in spite of the hierarchical nature of the nursing profession. It has also confronted nursing associations with the challenge of choosing between professionalism and unionization as the principal means for improving the nurse's status. (p. 26)

The nurses' problem is, of course, not unique. For instance, in the case of the Association of American University Professors (A.A.U.P.), a U.S. Supreme Court decision in 1980 concluded that because faculty members represented in university senate have decision-making authority in areas of budget, programs, and personnel, faculty members as a whole can be considered to be management-level employees and prevented from unionizing. As a result of this decision several U.S. college unions lost their collective bargaining rights (Todd, 1985); a trend which shows no evidence of slowing. This has had a calamitous effect on the academic librarians who saw the pursuit of faculty status as the best means by which they could achieve their goals. By claiming the rights of their faculty colleagues as their own (even though they seldom received the same benefits in actuality), many of the academic librarians who worked in unionized settings have lost their right to engage in collective bargaining.

A situation similar to that which beset the A.A.U.P. would face the library associations if they attempted to act as collective bargaining agents for library workers because they would be open to a charge of conflict of interest due to the large number of managerial-level librarians who actively participate in them. In order for a group, such as the

A.L.A., to assume a collective bargaining role, then, its membership would have to change considerably, although simply by assuming such a role the loss of the association's connections to the managerial contingent would probably be inevitable. When the U.S. National Education Association became a collective bargaining agent for teachers, for example, the associations representing management-level employees within the teaching hierarchy, such as school administrators and principals, ended their affiliation with the N.E.A. (Todd, 1985).

Todd (Ibid.) also pointed out out another barrier to collective bargaining that the A.L.A. would face.

> Since public employee bargaining is controlled by state law, the state organizations need to be the focus for bargaining activity. The small size of many state organizations. . . would have made it impossible to support a collective bargaining staff financially. The variability of state laws would have made nationally centralized bargaining impossible. Even if ALA had voted to accept collective bargaining, not every state association would automatically have supported this view. And since state associations are not bound by ALA decisions on issues affecting their geographic areas, they could refuse to undertake a collective bargaining role if they opposed it. (p. 291)

Despite the significance of these various barriers to collective bargaining, there is, however, an even more fundamental reason for the reluctance of the library associations to become embroiled in the so-called "bread-and-butter" issues of employment. Basically, "library associations have tended to co-opt employers rather than act as bargaining agents for librarians in negotiations with employers" (Reeves, 1980, p. 7). For instance, included among their members are public library trustees who are the actual employers of a large number of library workers. In other words, the employers' interests are heavily represented in the operation of the library associations. This rather unusual position is evident in the *1990/1991 ALA Handbook of Organization* (1990) in which it indicates that "the ALA will promote the recruitment, education, professional development, rights, interests and obligations of library personnel *and trustees*" (p. 235; emphasis mine).

As a result of this mixed membership and mandate, associations, such as the A.L.A., have been unable to develop any coherent policies with respect to employment issues. This can be easily seen in the A.L.A.'s rather awkward, straddling posture in relation to managers and workers. For example, in 1977, the A.L.A.'s executive director indicated that the association should become more active in defining the conditions of library employment, *while at the same time assisting library management*. Similarly, the association's statement on collective bargaining amounts, essentially, to a nonpolicy, representing neither the interests of managers nor those of library workers:

The American Library Association recognizes the principle of collective bargaining as one of the methods of conducting labor-management relations used by private and public institutions. The Association affirms the right of eligible employees to organize and bargain collectively with their employers, or to refrain from organizing and bargaining, without fear of reprisal. (1990 ALA Yearbook, p. 260)

Similar evidence of waffling over management versus workers' interests shows up in the A.L.A.'s policy regarding the dissemination of salary information. Although the association regularly gathers salary data, it leaves it up to "other individuals or groups to use the information. . . collected in support of their own goals" (Todd, 1985, p. 291). Reflected in this rather obscure statement is the association's complete lack of willingness to assume any responsibility for resolving salary inequities or, for that matter, even identifying them. A similar lack of attention to questions of remuneration is also evident in the other library associations. For instance, in his analysis of the future of academic librarianship, Veaner (1985) observed that the prestigious Association of College and Research Libraries had no mechanism through which compensation issues could be examined.

Pay Equity

Because the library associations are not only composed of a large number of management-level librarians, but their employers as well, it is nearly impossible for them to generate coherent policies on compensation that will not alienate significant numbers of their constituents. To understand the magnitude of this problem, it is useful to consider the role of the provincial library association during a recent attempt to implement pay equity legislation in the province of Ontario.

The intent of the 1987 Ontario Pay Equity Act was to allow for comparisons of salaries in male- and female-dominated job classes within individual "establishments." The ambiguous wording of the Act with respect to the definition of "employer" posed particular difficulties for the public library community in the province. Given the semi-autonomy of library boards relative to their host municipalities as defined under the provincial legislation governing public libraries, it was unclear who, exactly, was the public library worker's employer within the context of the pay equity legislation. In other words, it was unclear whether the comparisons of library workers' job classes were to be made within individual library systems or within the broader municipal framework.

Feminist groups and unions representing public library workers lobbied strenuously in favor of a solution to this dilemma which would define the municipality as the employer in this situation. Clearly, such a solution would have favored the library workers because it would have allowed for a comparison between the female-dominated job classes in libraries and the various male-dominated job classes within the municipalities. Despite widespread support for this solution, however, some library trustees as well as the senior managers of some of the largest public library systems in the province objected, arguing instead that the library boards should be defined as the employer (see Harris, 1988).

There seemed to be two motives behind this objection. First, the trustees were alarmed by the suggestion that the autonomy of the library boards might be challenged. Second, and more importantly, concern was expressed over the cost of paying the higher salaries to library workers that would have inevitably resulted from the pay equity adjustments. Many of the trustees, library directors, and municipal administrators grumbled over the cost of implementing the plan—clearly indicating that they were entirely too aware that library employees are, indeed, compensated at a very low rate in comparison with their counterparts in male-dominated occupations.[4]

At stake in this situation was the opportunity to compare the salaries paid to most classes of library workers (nearly all of which are female-dominated) to comparable classes of municipal workers, many of which are male-dominated. Thus, the salaries paid to librarians, for example, could be compared with those paid to urban planners and city engineers —job classes that require similar levels of education and responsibility. On the other hand, if the library boards were judged to be the employers, library workers could be compared only to other library workers and in many library systems there were no male-dominated job classes (with the exception of caretakers and van drivers in some of the larger systems). As a result, with no comparisons possible, there would be no opportunity to implement any adjustments in order to achieve pay equity and, of course, there would be no additional costs to the employer.

The role of the Ontario Library Association (O.L.A.) during this dispute was undistinguished. While the association did submit a brief in support of the legislation when it was first being drafted, it maintained a curious silence when the legislation was implemented. After some delay, a lobby group within the O.L.A. brought forward a resolution at a general meeting to support the idea of the municipality as employer for the purposes of the pay equity legislation. Although the resolution was passed, the execu-

---

[4] The whole debate over comparable worth is an ongoing one. As Galloway (1985) observed, the opponents of pay equity fail to understand that the mere fact that a woman does something leads it to be valued lower and compensated at a lower rate. Rather, they take the position that market forces control rates of pay (see, for example, O'Neill, 1985). In other words, when needed workers are in short supply their wages go up. However, one need only look at the current nursing shortage to realize that this is not the case, at least not when it comes to women's work.

tive did little to act on it and, as a result, smaller groups formed outside the association to work on the issue. In fact, in the year following the resolution, a motion to censure the O.L.A.'s executive for failing to act on the pay equity issue was only narrowly defeated.

In this province, the pay equity legislation represented a tremendous opportunity to improve the salary levels of library workers. The failure of the provincial association to respond to this opportunity was a reflection of the conflict of interest inherent in its membership. It demonstrated, clearly, the inability of the library associations to develop and act on employee-centered policies. The O.L.A., instead of playing a leadership role in this situation, gave a mixed and ineffectual message to the provincial government. As a result, no systematic resolution has been achieved to the dilemma facing public library workers. The pay equity process has evolved in a completely haphazard fashion across the province with public library workers being included in some municipal pay equity plans and excluded in others.

LIBRARY UNIONS

The pay equity example clearly illustrates the conflict of interest vis-à-vis employees, managers, and employers in which the library associations would be placed if they were to take on the role of collective bargaining agent. Not only would they have to undergo a major shift in their membership structure, but they would also have to win over those library workers who have already joined other unions. As Todd (1985) pointed out, even if the A.L.A. had been interested in assuming the role of collective bargaining agent and was able to overcome the various obstacles it would have faced in doing so, by 1970 it was too late. Without the associations to bargain for them, library workers had already become involved in a variety of different types of unions. Thus, "although union activity continued during the seventies, ALA had already missed its chance to get in on the ground floor of unionization" (Ibid., p. 290).

The unions presented library workers with an alternative to associations; however, they, too, pose a particular set of problems for their members. For example, when library workers form their own unions they may be unable to succeed in their demands by using work stoppage as a tactic. In this respect they have simply not got the same leverage available to other, more powerful unions. This problem has also faced other small groups such as the hospital technicians who, in attempting to unionize in a fashion similar to that of the nurses, "have largely failed, because their numbers are too small and the skills can be bought elsewhere" (Brown, 1975, p. 181).

According to Brown (1975), the nurses were successful in unionizing because they have enough members in their occupation "in positions that can bring hospitals to a halt" (p. 181). While librarians and other library workers could also, in all likelihood, bring their libraries to a halt, it is questionable whether the absence of library service would have the same immediate impact on public opinion as the shutdown of hospital services. "While short-term inconvenience would result if these occupations were to strike, severe dislocation would not result from interruption or delay in the provision of their services" (Wilson, 1982, p. 185).

For library workers, the alternative to forming their own unions is to belong to unions in which several different kinds of employees are represented, particularly since there is some indication that "multi-professional units" are favored as bargaining agents in labor legislation. Dolan (1980) observed that for nurses, for example, such units will become the norm unless they "can demonstrate that their interests are so disparate with other professional groups that their interests will not be fairly represented" (p. 52). The advantage of such mixed units is that they are more powerful because of the combined threat of work stoppage by large numbers of employees. However, they also pose some drawbacks.

In mixed units in which library workers are included with workers from a variety of different occupations, librarians often find that their interests are not particularly well looked after. In collective bargaining arrangements with universities, for example, librarians with faculty status are likely to comprise only a small percentage of the bargaining unit for academic employees (although, as noted earlier, this may all become somewhat of a moot point in the United States if the trend to decertify faculty unions continues). As a result, their concerns are not likely to be taken up by the whole group. For instance, when the librarians at the State University of New York learned that their needs had been neglected in a contract, the response of their union was that "it could not accomplish everything for everyone and librarians must consider themselves part of the whole and go along with greatest good for the greatest number" (Commerton, 1975, p. 132). Similar problems have been encountered by social workers who, when they do belong to unions, tend to be found in large, mixed unions that represent a variety of workers. Humphreys and Dinerman (1984) observed that "these broad-based unions tend to push issues and agendas that rarely reflect solely or principally the needs or interests of social workers" (p. 210).

Given the advantages and disadvantages in both arrangements, are library workers better off in unions that embrace a variety of employees from different occupations or in those which represent only librarians and other library employees? At present, the answer to this is unclear. According to O'Reilly and O'Reilly (1981), the "research, which is sparse, does not indicate that either one of the opportunities delivers more advantages than the other" (p. 107). On the other hand, Mudge (1986) reported that

> the larger the unit the more effective its members are in obtaining what they want at the bargaining table. Consequently, it behooves librarians to join as large a bargaining unit as possible. This could mean joining with support staff or with faculty members to become more powerful at negotiation time. (p. 194)

As to whether or not there is any advantage to bargaining units which include librarians as well as nonprofessional library workers, Mudge (Ibid.) noted that "librarians are outnumbered in any bargaining unit containing support staff; therefore, any issues important to librarians could receive a low priority at the bargaining table" (p. 193). In fact, she found no differences between certified bargaining units in academic and public libraries in the achievement of such things as salaries, benefits, hours of work, vacations, and job descriptions, regardless of whether these units were composed of staff only, librarians only, or included both. However, when it came to achieving such things as career development clauses, contracting-out provisions, paid conference leaves, paid association memberships, peer evaluations, representation on library committees, travel funds, and tenure clauses "bargaining units consisting only of librarians were the most successful and mixed units the least so" (p. 194).[5]

Although it is interesting to consider the relative advantages of different types of union arrangements for library workers, those who have pinned their hopes to collective bargaining as a means of achieving their occupational goals must face some harsh realities. With the decertification of faculty unions and a generally chilly climate for union activity of any description in the United States, it seems unlikely that unionization will solve the salary and status problems of librarianship, at least not in the near future. Therefore, it is important to consider, once again, the roles that are to be played by the library associations in the development of the profession.

THE PROFESSIONAL ASSOCIATIONS

Because of their problematic membership configurations, Boissonnas (1972) concluded that library associations, such as the A.L.A., are not true professional associations. Indeed, relative to more powerful associations, such as the American Medical Association, the A.L.A. is weak and

---

[5] Mudge's (1984) findings are of particular importance to librarians who work in public libraries since they are normally organized in mixed bargaining units.

has even had some difficulty in regulating entry into the field. For instance, even though all the M.L.S. programs offered in library schools in Canada are accredited by the A.L.A., this is not true in the United States. According to the *1989–90 Directory Issue* of the Association of Library and Information Science Education, 20 percent of American library, information science, and school media graduate programs are not accredited (13 of 65 schools).

Nevertheless, despite such difficulties, the library associations are important in maintaining a sense of unity in the field. As Winter (1988) put it,

> the very heterogeneity of the occupation seems to exert a counteracting force toward unity, and in fact we find a consistent reliance throughout the profession (with the possible exception of school librarianship...) on central associations and professional education programs. This suggests the great importance of the associations and the schools in supplying and then reinforcing some of the group cohesion that is lost in the development of subspecialties and types of work setting. Clearly the occupation has become more specialized in recent years and will no doubt continue in this direction. And this in turn suggests that the associations and the schools will have, if anything, an even greater responsibility to provide a shared sense of professional identity. (p. 65)

He argued, for instance, that the A.L.A. has helped to maintain this sense of identity by providing definitions of professional, paraprofessional, and clerical library work. Furthermore, since 1970, it has encouraged "lobbying, public relations campaigns, and the marketing of professional services as additional means of preserving control" (Ibid., p. 90). This public relations aspect of the A.L.A.'s work became particularly intense when the M.L.S. began to face serious challenges as the minimum qualification for entry into professional positions. Here, however, one can again see the difficulties faced by a group with such a mixed membership and confused agenda and, despite Winter's optimism, the effectiveness of the A.L.A.'s performance in the public relations arena has, at least to date, been somewhat less than spectacular.

The A.L.A.'s Support for Professional Education

In 1970 the A.L.A. endorsed the principle of the master's degree as the basic requirement for employment as a librarian (Holley, 1984). However, not too long afterward it became evident that this was to be at odds with growing movement in the United States to challenge the minimum requirements for jobs. Since then, the A.L.A.'s position on the matter of minimum qualifications has been, at best, equivocal. In 1980, the association's Office for Library Personnel Resources suggested that the M.L.S. "represents not a requirement but an ideal" (Ibid., p. 327). This position was consistent with the A.L.A.'s refusal to get involved in the famous Merwine case in which a woman who held in master's degree in education sued the Mississippi State University for failing to hire her for a position as a librarian. Oddly enough, the A.L.A.'s failure to take a stand in favor of the M.L.S. during the Merwine case was not at all consistent with its rather spirited response to the U.S. federal government's proposal in 1982 to reclassify (i.e., downgrade) librarian positions. Making another about face, the association's position in this case was that the M.L.S. should be considered a basic requirement for the federal occupational class of "professional librarian." This flip-flopping on the part of the association did not go unnoticed. Edward Holley, then a library school dean, was called on to testify as an expert witness during the Merwine case. He commented that it "flies in the face of logic and common sense for ALA to fight vigorously before the U.S. Office of Personnel Management and not fight strongly for the MLS degree in the federal courts. The actions are mutually contradictory" (p. 330). The rather weak language describing the A.L.A.'s present position on this issue indicates an ongoing ambivalence with respect to professional education. The *1990/1991 ALA Handbook of Organization* states that the A.L.A. "supports the provision of library services by professionally qualified personnel who have been educated in graduate programs within institutions of higher education" (p. 261).

UNIONS AND ASSOCIATIONS: CAN THEY COEXIST?

Despite the problems the library associations experience in responding consistently to employee-centered issues, they do fulfill some important functions within the field. They provide some unity in the increasingly fragmented information sector and address, at least to some degree, the difficult problem of domain protection. As such, they are likely to play a continuing role in the field. The question remains, however, as to how they might most effectively coexist with whatever remains of the unions to which library workers belong.

Wilson (1984) argued that the associations' role vis-à-vis employment of librarians is a "non issue," observing that

> we all acknowledge that the purpose of a union is to protect the economic interests of its members. . . . Not so widely acknowledged is the fact that this is also one of the purposes of the professional association. (p. 564)

She pointed out that while unions achieve this goal by using the threat of work stoppage, the associations use other tactics including government lobbying, the supervision of education, and setting standards for service and entry into the profession. Through all these activities the associations' goals are to "to improve the market for members by making them and their service better and thus more highly valued" (p. 564).

Making a similar point, Biblarz, Capron, Kennedy, Ross, and Weinerth (1975) suggested that both unions and associations have necessary roles to play in the profession and they differ only in emphasis. In other words, while the unions attend to the immediate concerns of the membership, such as wages and working conditions, the associations should concentrate on long-term issues that affect the field as a whole.

Taking this one step further, some have argued that the library associations should "assume more of the functions of the learned society and fewer of the trade association" (Winter, 1988, p. 110). Others, on the other hand, have suggested that the associations should take an advisory role with respect to the unions in which librarians are represented. Based on her experience with more broadly based academic unions in which the particular concerns of librarians may be overlooked, Commerton (1975) recommended that "the associations, as collective units, must be the agencies to give proper information and advice to the unions. They must apply constant pressure and demand to be heard" (p. 134). However, given the membership configuration of the library associations and the potential for conflict between the managerial and nonmanagerial members, one wonders how likely they would be to assume such a role.

Changing the Library Associations

If they are ever to become effective in representing their members, the library associations must make several significant changes. First, they must decide on their constituency. At present, the membership includes anyone (as well as institutions). While this broadens their financial base, it also makes it very difficult for the associations to develop policies that members can stand behind. Todd (1985) was fundamentally correct when she argued that the A.L.A. was wise to avoid the pitfalls facing other professional associations that have engaged in collective bargaining on behalf of their members. However, even if it continues to eschew collective bargaining, the A.L.A. (and the other library associations) could play a much stronger role as an advocate for library workers, but only if a decision is taken that its mandate is, indeed, to represent library workers.

Focusing on a particular constituency within the library community would enable the associations to develop policies which could be consistently expressed during lobbying efforts. Furthermore, through the expression of such policies, particularly if they were to be employee-centered, the associations should be able not only to identify other groups with similar interests, but to forge links with these groups. In this respect, Hash's (1982) advice (albeit advice to nurses) is particularly relevant:

In order to play an effective role in politics, nurses, like any other group, must first organize for the task and then seek to act in a unified and consistent fashion. Nurses have already accomplished much of the organizational task through structures like the National League for Nursing and the American Nurses Association. An equally important task is the continuing need to coordinate efforts within the profession and with other organizations that share common views. . . . While nursing may never speak with one voice, it is important for the profession to seek the broadest possible base of support for its attempt to influence politics. (p. 5)

Low status, lack of compensation, and the desire for greater autonomy are issues of common concern to all the female-intensive occupations and all are readily understood within a feminist analysis of work. Just as Weibel (1976) suggested some years ago that it is time for library workers to become organized participants in the women's movement, now it is time, more than ever, for organizations, such as the A.L.A., to become feminist associations.

PART II

Environmental Pressures Affecting Librarianship

It would be foolish to undertake an analysis of any occupation without considering the external environment in which it operates. In the remaining chapters two of the forces that are altering the nature of librarianship are examined. Rapid advances in computing technology, for example, as well as the growth in the service and information sectors of the economy have both had a tremendous impact on the field. Indeed, as will be seen in Chapter 7, as a result of its growing reliance on automated systems, library work is being significantly altered as is the composition of the library labor force. Increasingly, experts from outside the field are being imported to assume significant technical and administrative roles while the core professional tasks of librarianship are being redefined and, in some cases, deskilled. And, as should become apparent in Chapter 8, all this is taking place within a turbulent economic environment in which control over information is shifting rapidly away from libraries and into the private sector where it is seen as a commodity to be bought and sold.

At first glance, neither of these topics may seem to qualify as "women's" issues. Yet, when one looks closely, it is apparent that both automation and the growing information sector of the economy have had a significant impact on the very nature of women's work in librarianship and pose a serious threat to the future of the field. As will be discussed in Chapter 9, the uncertain future of librarianship suggests an urgent need to reexamine what is valued in this field.

CHAPTER 7

Technology and the Deskilling of Women's Work

One of the truisms about the workplace is that it is segregated by gender. Not only do women and men tend to be clustered in different occupations, but within these fields they are segregated into different subareas. As noted in earlier chapters, the female-intensive occupations offer no exception to this rule. In fact, men are found in senior administrative positions in numbers disproportionate to their total presence in these fields.

In librarianship, there is some evidence that a disproportionately large number of men work (and study) in areas of the field in which the primary emphasis is computer technology, whereas women are overrepresented in areas such as children's librarianship and cataloging (see, for example, Harris, Monk, and Austin, 1986; Harris, Michell, and Cooley, 1985; Harris and Reid, 1988). Given this pattern, it may be no coincidence that it is in just these areas that U.S. libraries are currently having the greatest difficulty recruiting trained employees (Heim, 1988). At one time, bright women had relatively few options available to them if they chose to pursue careers. Today, however, librarianship is in competition with dozens of other attractive occupations, many of which offer the promise of greater salaries and more prestige. And, within the field itself, relative to areas such as cataloging or children's work, the so-called "male specialties" are generally accorded higher status (Harris, Monk, and Austin, 1986).

With the prominent and ever-changing role of automated systems in the field of librarianship, the patterns of work in this occupation have changed dramatically. As a result, it appears that some of the female areas of specialization, especially cataloging, are undergoing a process of "de-professionalization" or "deskilling." A decade ago Schiller (1981) observed that, in contrast to traditional arrangements, when libraries began to contract with external suppliers for online information or online cataloguing service, they thereby became intermediaries in a much larger, and very different kind of informational system, with impacts on library services to users, collections, staff, organizations, and support that have only begun to be seen. (p. 709)

Some of these impacts have indeed become more evident and, according to Hafter (1986), "technology may provide the foundation for both the information society and the deprofessionalization of the information profession" (p. 53).

THE DESKILLING OF INFORMATION WORK

That the deskilling trend has been especially damaging to women in this profession has seldom been addressed directly in library literature. Vagianos and Lesser (1988) did warn that women may be especially vulnerable to technological displacement in the information sector. Similarly chilling, especially for library workers who are employed at the clerical and paraprofessional levels, is Webster and Robins's (1986) observation that "because women disproportionately work in low-skilled, most often white-collar occupations where they deal routinely with information...their labor has every likelihood of being automated" (p. 163). Comments such as these, however, are rare in the vast array of published material on the impact of the new technologies on library and information work.

In a discussion of the future of libraries, Vagianos and Lesser (1988) described two types of information workers: "knowledge workers" who create information and "data workers" who use or process information. Data workers, the larger of the two groups, carry out a variety of jobs including "all of the lowest skill, routine, clerical type jobs" (p. 36). According to these authors,

women are proportionately better represented in the data worker versus knowledge worker sector and thus may continue to be subject to the traditional, nontechnological barriers to advancement characteristic of their labor market position up to now. Moreover, women may be more likely to be negatively influenced by technological displacement of workers. (p. 36)

The displacement and the deskilling of certain aspects of information work has profound implications for librarians. In fact, Kraft (1987) reported that unlike all other occupational groups in the information sector, the number of library workers in the United States actually decreased during the mid-1980s, a decline which, according to Kraft, "may be computer related" (p. 131).

DEPROFESSIONALIZATION

Sociologist Nina Toren (1975) described a variety of ways by which a profession may lose its status including loss of "exclusive mastery" over a knowledge base, declining importance of a profession's services, loss of the service ideal, and failure to retain a "legal monopoly over admission, training, licensing, and judgement of performance" (p. 326). With the increased use of automated systems in many professions, much of the work in these fields is becoming routinized. And, as Toren (Ibid.) explained, "one of the strongest foundations on which professions base their claim to autonomy and monopoly is the dictum that professional work is nonroutine" (p. 329). What is increasingly happening in the professions, however, is that

> the processes of specialization, standardization, and routinization of problems and their solutions make professional work less complicated and uncertain, and more precise, efficient, reliable, and fair. It also allows for the delegation of routine activities to less qualified personnel leaving the complex and difficult problems to the trained professional. Sometimes, however, not much is left to warrant a distinct professional status and its correlates. (p. 330)

The other threat to professionalism, according to Toren (Ibid.), is related to the service ideal.

> The professional-client relationship has been traditionally governed by the former's claim to autonomy (freedom from lay control), and authority (the client's duty to obey), by virtue of his superior knowledge and dedication to service the client's best interests. . . . Standardization and routinization make professional activities more comprehensible to outsiders, and consequently subject to their evaluation and control. (p. 332)

Thus, she argued, "the two fundamental sources of deprofessionalization arise from the core characteristics of a profession—its knowledge base and the service ideal" (p. 335).[1] Toren's model is particularly useful for examining the fortunes of occupations, such as librarianship, for, as will become evident in the following sections, the pressures of deprofessionalization are evident in a number of the female-intensive fields.

The Declassification of Social Workers

The perception that social work involves little more than listening and giving advice gives rise to the idea that anyone can do it. This has con-

---

[1] Clearly, Toren's (1975) model, even though extremely useful for conceptualizing the decline of the professions, should be viewed with some caution as it relies heavily on the trait model of professionalism.

tributed to "a wholesale attempt to 'declassify' social work as a profession, an initiative started by the Nixon Administration" (Humphreys and Dinerman, 1984, p. 199). This initiative, largely motivated by cost cutting, removes specific educational requirements for social work jobs. Essentially, declassification reduces personnel costs in social service programs by replacing graduate social workers with less qualified staff. Thus, jobs that at one time required at least the B.S.W. may no longer require even a university degree. According to Siporin (1984), in the United States

> there has been a definite trend to restrict the number of social work positions in federal, state and local agencies and to curtail the employment of professional social workers. Along with the fiscal crisis, the declassification movement, in which agencies fill social work jobs with personnel who do not have social work educational qualifications, has meant the loss of many social work positions. It also has made for substantial unemployment among social workers. . . . Social work services may be needed as much or more than ever, but increasingly they are being provided by non-social work 'human service workers,' new demiprofessionals, such as 'drug counsellors,' and by professionals from other disciplines in what is an increasingly competitive arena. (p. 238)

The declassification of social work has led to a much more profound erosion of the profession than that which was anticipated by many social workers who were, at one time, preoccupied with questions, such as the relative merit of the B.S.W. versus the M.S.W. degrees. For instance, Dyer (1977) recognized the conflict between professionalism and efficiency when he observed that

> many practitioners question the professional status of BSW workers and view the extension of such status to anyone with less than a master's degree as retarding the professionalization process and lowering the status of the profession. Opposing this view are the agencies that employ the workers. These agencies are generally organized around bureaucratic principles that emphasize efficiency. 'Good' employees are those who can accomplish the functions for the agency in the most efficient way. (p. 487)

Clearly, however, Dyer (Ibid.) did not anticipate just how far this efficiency argument was going to be taken in his field.

In some jurisdictions, as a result of the declassification movement, one does not need a degree of any sort to do work that was once considered professional. Furthermore, over the last two decades the downgrading of educational requirements for some social work positions has been accompanied by the introduction of automated record-keeping systems into many welfare departments. Garson (1988) observed that family assistance workers who perform jobs that at one time would have earned them the title of social worker

> no longer need a college degree and they're paid less than social workers. Because Welfare has been automating piecemeal and because it's a civil service job, more employees stay on. Therefore, we're able for once to watch some individuals move down steadily, step by step, from autonomous professionals to skilled clerks. (p. 110)

Reclassifying Library Workers

As noted several times in earlier chapters, the standard for entry to practice librarianship has been the focus of some dispute within the field. While most professional positions in U.S. and Canadian libraries require at least the M.L.S., there are, according to Winter (1988), "continuing challenges to this requirement, both from within the ALA and from a combination of external social and legal forces" (p. 88). The most serious of these challenges was the U.S. federal government's proposal during the early 1980s to revise the classification and qualification standards for librarians, library technicians, and information specialists (see Robinson, 1983; Stephens, 1986). Although the threatened changes to the classification scheme were never actually carried out, the U.S. Office of Personnel Management, which opposes "excessive credentialing," does not require the M.L.S. from candidates for federal library jobs nor does the Library of Congress, which employs thousands of library workers.

In a move similar to that undertaken by the American government, the Canadian federal government has proposed a new classification scheme for public servants in which librarians would be reclassified within a new "Administrative" category. Formerly part of the "Scientific and Professional" employee category, members of the library science group are the only employees within this category to lose their identity as a professional group. According to the National Library of Canada's response to the recommended restructuring, with the exception of the library group, "all the proposed new groupings involving groups from the Scientific and Professional Category consist either exclusively or predominantly of scientific and professional groups" (National Library of Canada, 1990, p. 1). "By contrast, the Library Science group is to be absorbed into a huge and predominantly non-professional group, over 50 percent of which is to be made up from groups currently in the Administrative Support Category" (Ibid., p. 2). Recognizing that this proposed restructuring is, indeed, a women's issue, the National Library's response points out that librarianship is female-dominated and that this plan "will place yet another female-dominated group into a burgeoning ghetto" (Ibid.).

A related question raised by this new proposal is that of pay equity. Sadly, it seems that hardfought battles, thought to be won years ago, are facing Canadian librarians once again. In 1982, the Canadian Human Rights Commission

> determined that the work performed by those in the female-dominated Library Science Group is equal in value to that performed by those in the predominantly male Historical Research Group. As a result of that decision the Library Science Group currently receives equalization payments as a means of providing equity with the Historical Research Group. The proposed restructuring will inevitably skew once again the pay plans for librarians and historical researchers. (Ibid., p. 3)

Salaries in the Administrative Category would range from $15,000 to $70,000, while those in the proposed Research class would range between $18,000 and $82,000. Clearly, the proposal to include the Library Science Group in the Administrative category reflects not only a lack of understanding about the nature of library work, but signals, once again, the belief that women's work is of less value than men's and that the notion of a woman's "profession" is a logical contradiction.

The Deprofessionalizing of Cataloging Work

The routinization of work through automation has had a major impact on the activities of cataloging librarians who at one time performed what many would consider to be *the* core function of the profession. The changing nature of the cataloger's work illustrates Toren's (1975) idea that deprofessionalization can occur when a field loses control over its knowledge base. In the case of catalogers, this loss of control has come about largely because of the widespread use of cataloging networks or bibliographic utilities, that is, services that provide libraries with access to online databases containing millions of cataloging records. Through such services, libraries need no longer do original cataloging on site for most materials. Instead, they can simply purchase the cataloging records they need already prepared. In a study of the role of catalogers in academic libraries Hafter (1986) found that since the introduction of network cataloging some 80 to 98 percent of cataloging is now processed from network copy by library assistants. This led her to conclude that "most network documentation and the activities resulting from that documentation are based on a clerical, not a professional, knowledge base" (p. 74).

The use of cataloging networks not only shifts most of the in-house cataloging work in libraries to nonprofessional staff, but it also alters the working patterns of the remaining professional catalogers. According to Hafter (1986), in the past, catalogers usually specialized in subject or language areas, reviewed all the materials acquired in those areas and cataloged both the 'hot' items (to get them in circulation quickly) and the difficult ones. . . . Now . . . the cataloger has to work in several subjects areas because there are not enough items that require original cataloging in most disciplines to warrant subject specialization. Therefore, the professional loses mastery over the literature in a given area. This loss of control and knowledge slows the cataloger. Thus, the catalogers have to exert extra effort just to maintain their previous production statistics. Working on the material now left in the backlog also requires increased psychological effort. It is sometimes of very limited local interest. (p. 72)

With the reduction in the need for original cataloging, Hafter (Ibid.) found that there was an overall decline in the size of the cataloging departments in the libraries in her sample.

In general, fewer professional catalogers were employed. . . . Even in those departments that suffered little or no attrition in the number of professional positions, it was clear that the role and career expectations of the cataloger had greatly diminished. (p. 63)

There is mixed evidence at present as to whether this trend has been continuing. While some authors point to the difficulties in recruiting and retaining catalogers in the United States (see, for example, Bishoff, 1989; Neal, 1989), a senior manager in a large public library system told me recently that *no* catalogers had been hired in her system for more than eight years.

Even those who argue that the need for professional catalogers is as critical now as it has ever been agree that the nature of these jobs has changed. Bishoff (1989), for example, noted that catalogers are needed "to fill their traditional role of original cataloging, department management and staff training, as well as new responsibilities in system administration, design and system analysis" (p. 42). Similarly Neal (1989), who claimed that "libraries are increasingly facing unprecedented difficulties in recruiting and retaining professional catalogers," acknowledged that many of these positions involve "a significant non-cataloging component" (p. 113). In fact, like Hafter (1986), Neal (1989) recognized that

as bibliographic processes have been automated and turned over to an increasingly clerical workflow, catalogers have faced far more limited scope for the use of full bibliographic skills and subject/language expertise. (p. 114)

Just as with the routinization and downgrading of certain types of social work, the major force behind the reduction in the numbers of professional catalogers in libraries is an economic one. As Hafter (1986) put it,

the need to control finances and to provide new services (many of them computer and/or network based) forces administrators to consider ways to reallo-
cate resources. Cataloging is an expensive, labor-intensive activity which
many administrators feel can no longer be justified. (p. 55)

This reallocation of resources moves the control over technical services
work away from catalogers and toward administrators and systems analysts. Senior catalogers formerly

determined workflow and set production quotas, goals, and standards,
working in consultation with other catalogers and other members of the
libary administration. In the automated systems, network computer availability affected scheduling while system analysts and non-cataloging administrators began to exert more influence over setting production standards.
(p. 64)

Thus, as Estabrook (1983) explained, the "substitution of computerized
for manual systems provides increased opportunities for managerial control over the pace and nature of work" (p. 74). Of course, this phenomenon
is not only evident in librarianship. Rather, it has been observed in a variety
of work settings ranging from the preparation of hamburgers in fast food
restaurants to the output of secretaries and stock brokers (Garson, 1988).

Hildenbrand (1989b) argued that what she termed "the crisis in cataloging" is related to "the identification of cataloging as 'women's work'
within librarianship" (p. 217). While she acknowledged that there are
inadequate data to determine positively that women are overrepresented
in professional cataloging, she did cite some evidence which suggests that
catalogers trail other types of librarians in status and salary. And, in fact,
as more and more of the cataloging work in libraries becomes clerical, it
does, indeed, increasingly become women's work. Given this pattern, it is
important to note that those who work as administrators and systems
analysts, specialties in the field in which men are overrepresented, set the
standards as well as control and monitor the work that is largely undertaken by women. As is typical of women's work generally, cataloging has
been ignored and undervalued (except by other catalogers, of course) at
the expense of libraries and their users. The short-sightedness of this view
has already had a negative impact on the field. The failure to use catalogers in the design of some information retrieval systems has led to inconsistency, redundancy, and missing information in some databases. As
Whittaker (1988) put it,

you can have an outstanding collection, marvellous reference librarians, and
a top-of-the-line circulation system, but if you don't have the vital link of
bibliographic control (unless your collection numbers only a couple of hun-

dred titles), there is no way to get the appropriate items into the hands of the interested patron. Catalogers and the records they create provide that link. (p. 12)

As more people begin to recognize that without the input of trained catalogers libraries face the possibility of losing bibliographic control, there is an increasing concern expressed in the literature about the trend observed in some of the library schools to drop cataloging as a required course from the M.L.S. curriculum. Hayes (1989) noted, for instance, that while it may be efficient to use clerical and/or technical staff to carry out a large amount of cataloging,

> those staff must be supervised by professionals who know what is needed. The basic data, as generated by the Library of Congress and the major resource libraries of the country, must be created by professionals. The range of materials and differing formats for them that need to be cataloged is steadily increasing; each of them requires the highest level of professional qualification. (p. 5)

Over the years, Hayes, a well-known information scientist, has become increasingly convinced about the importance of cataloging. In fact, he has argued that knowledge of cataloging is "essential to information systems analysis and design, and not simply in terms of library applications" (p. 9). He even went so far as to describe cataloging as

> *the fundamental basis for a theory to our field.* It is here that information organization and structure become identified and the means for handling them specified. The structures embodied in cataloging are the basis for all subsequent retrieval, including reference. Even the substantive tasks in library management revolve around the structure provided by the catalog. (p. 10; emphasis mine).

Claiming that the foundations of cataloging are essential to understanding all database design problems, Hayes urged that it "be required of all students, whatever their level and whatever their specialty, including information science" (p. 15).

CHANGING ROLES IN LIBRARIANSHIP

Are the difficulties that have faced catalogers likely to be encountered by other types of librarians? Buckland (1989) predicted that with increased automation another traditionally key function of professional librarians— collection development—will diminish in importance. In contrast, Hafter

(1986) observed that the status of systems and reference librarians had increased (presumably because of the status-enhancing effect of associating with computers). Nevertheless, she warned that this work too "may be capable of being restructured into smaller and simpler components and automated" (p. 130).

Online searching is an aspect of reference librarianship that came into particular prominence during the 1970s. In the traditional model of online searching a library patron consulted with a librarian. Thus, "the online interview was, of necessity, centered on the intermediary, who was able to serve only a single user at a time" (Janke and Nicholls, in press, p. 1). Within this arrangement, Janke and Nicholls (in press) noted, the "users never really learn how to use the service. Only intermediaries search. Even when the system is visible onscreen to users, it remains inaccessible to them" (p. 2). While in the short run this form of online searching may have enhanced the status of reference librarians, as it casts them in the role of the expert vis-à-vis the patron, the technology may lead, eventually, to a situation reminiscent of the reshaping of the cataloging department. In other words, "if online searching can be construed as a technological advance systematizing hitherto esoteric professional knowledge, then librarianship may experience deprofessionalization in the future" (Nielsen, 1980, p. 218).

As more and more library users sought online search services during the late 1970s and early 1980s, some library managers expected to increase the staffing of the reference desk with nonprofessionals in order to free professional reference librarians for this specialty task (Nielsen, 1980). However, with the increasing use of technologies that enable people to conduct their own database searches (a process referred to as end-user searching), the role of the specialized online search librarian appears to be decreasing in significance. In Janke and Nicholls's opinion, the traditional model of online searching will become less and less important as end-users initiate their own contact with the databases in which they are interested. In fact, they noted that with the introduction of CD-ROM systems, "passive user reliance on librarians, as expert intermediaries who are in control of the search process, is already on the wane in the reference environment of most large academic libraries" (Ibid., p. 12).

Does the loss of the intermediary role in online searching and the staffing of general reference desks with nonprofessional staff signal the deprofessionalizing of the reference function? Not everyone thinks so. Not surprisingly, those who are strong advocates of the new information technologies see these changes as opportunities rather than losses. Janke and Nicholls (Ibid.), for instance, predicted that those who were once busy with online searching will now "adopt a more informal advisory role as counselor, reference, librarian, instructor and orientation librarian" (p. 9) in which they will "inevitably take on far greater responsibilities. . . than they ever conceivably could within the limitations of the traditional model" (p. 10). Hall (1984), too, argued that although the knowledge base of librarianship is being restructured and routinized as a result of automation, "it does not follow that the practice is being deprofessionalized" (p. 26). Instead, she suggested that even though

> the older type of librarian is being deskilled, other library skills are being developed or are being replaced by the high level skills of another profession. The reference or special librarian is now very highly skilled as are those devising computer systems. (p. 24)

Like Hall, Allen (1984) also made optimistic predictions about the future of librarianship. As the field absorbs the impact of automation, Allen (Ibid.) expects it to be the "catalyst that finally enables librarians to concentrate on the truly intellectual aspects of library operations and management" (p. 11).

The New Librarianship

Even those who are most optimistic about the new technologies acknowledge that in their vision of the future the direct service role formerly played by reference librarians will be deprofessionalized as nonprofessional staff assume primary responsibility for most patron contact. As Hall (1984) described it, users will become an "abstraction" for the professional librarians (and others) who design and manage information systems. For Hall then, the "new librarianship" is a field that responds to "a need that has been abstracted out of its original and particular context and is generalized to a sizeable user group" (Ibid., p. 23). However, what she described is not really a new librarianship, but basically a new occupation.

What will this occupation look like? Many futurists agree that the most significant roles remaining to librarians in the face of automation will be teaching and consulting. For instance, Veaner (1985) predicted that no matter what it is called in the future, there will still be an infrastructure that will "need librarians as intermediaries, teachers, consultants, advisers, and interpreters" (p. 228). Highlighting this teaching function, Taylor (1989) observed that with the end-user searching made available through CD-ROMs, this technology is "changing the nature of reference work. Reference librarians are spending hundreds of hours helping students and faculty use CD-ROMs" (p. 454). Similarly, Harter and Jackson (1988) predicted that if librarians are to have any role vis-à-vis optical disc technologies, it most likely will be as teachers and consultants. If anything is certain, it is that optical disc systems and large bibliographic and other databases will very soon be found in large numbers outside traditional libraries altogether. (p. 521)

Indeed, they suggested that the notion of a library as a particular place should be rethought

as being extended into faculty office areas or wherever an optical disc system may be located. Librarians in such libraries will need to be mobile, aggressive, and oriented toward education. In this sense optical discs can be viewed as being in direct competition with the library itself, at least as it is traditionally viewed. (p. 522)

Bearman (1987) also expected that the new technologies would inevitably lead to increased teaching and consulting roles.

Even with improved front end packages and enhanced expert systems, the proliferation of databases and the rapidly changing technologies will require the help of information professionals to keep up with services, provide expert access to them, and serve as a member of the organization's management planning team knowledgeable about information assets. (p. 84)

Making a similar point, Katz (1983) predicted that librarians will be "more involved with assisting the less-than-expert user with determining what bits of data will solve problems" (p. 369).

All this leads one to wonder, of course, whether limiting the roles of professional librarians to those of consulting and teaching users about the new technologies will not eventually result in the demise of the occupation since both functions are inherently short term in nature. As both software and its end-users become more and more sophisticated, the need for expert intermediaries will, presumably, shrink or at least appear to be less necessary as end-users become more convinced of the quality of their systems.[2] The cyclical nature of this process has already been evident in the fate of computer programmers. In fact, "programmers (who are, in effect, the deskillers since it their programs which embody the skill and judgment of the workers) are themselves subject to progressive deskilling" (Kraft, 1987, p. 32).

The changes which have been predicted in librarianship are not limited to function but extend, as well, to the actual labels given to the work.

---

[2] It is important to recognize, however, that many users of automated systems have been disappointed upon discovering the true capabilities of the technology. While there is no denying the speed with which they can transact simple transfer tasks, the performance of automated systems in complex retrieval functions has often fallen short of consumers' expectations.

According to Bearman (1987), "we can expect many companies and organizations in the next decade to include information assets in their strategic planning and to have a senior vice president for Information Resources Management" (p. 85). Similarly, Rowe (1987) predicted that in both universities and corporations a new role will emerge for the "Chief Information Officer" who will be "in charge of data-processing centers, records managements, archives, and communications" (p. 297) as well as libraries. In case librarians might be attracted to such a title, however, Rowe (Ibid.) also predicted that they "do not have much an edge in qualifying for that CIO role" (p. 297) because they have not restructured their roles or marketed themselves. In the face of such changes, then, the outlook for librarians looks somewhat gloomy even though Rowe did acknowledge that they are as well qualified as anyone else for these elaborate-sounding positions because "nobody knows more about making databases accessible and about interaction between users than librarians" (p. 297).

RENAMING WOMEN'S WORK

While the opportunity to take on these roles may pose an exciting challenge to librarians, it is worth keeping in mind that there can be only one senior vice president for information and one chief information officer in any organization. What jobs will remain to the librarians who do not compete successfully for these lucrative positions is perhaps more important to this discussion.

Parson (1984) described what he called "a new paradigm for librarianship" and suggested that librarians should

> shift away from their strict identification with the library as an agency or institution to an identification with the client or library user. Such a shift will enhance the effectiveness of the librarian as an information advocate or information-interpreting agent. (p. 372)

In a similar vein, Horton (1982) described the need for what he called an "information counselor" whose function would be to help the user interact with information suppliers and handlers. He distinguished this new role from those already performed by librarians by claiming that "traditionally, the librarian's role has been to assist rather than to do" (p. 17). According to Horton (Ibid.), this helping orientation

> virtually dooms many librarians who may *want* to become information managers, but whose skills, attitudes, and approach to their jobs keep them exclusively in a service, and so subordinate role. The information manager *must* concern himself with... whether information assets and resources are

used efficiently and effectively to achieve bottom-line results for the enterprise. (p. 18)

Whether or not one accepts arguments like those of Horton (Ibid.) and
others, it is clear that the pressures on librarians to rid themselves of their
occupational labels are intense.

In her discussion of deprofessionalization, Toren (1975) observed that
when engineers became alarmed at the routinization of certain aspects of
their work, some of them pursued managerial careers in order to increase
their status. From this she concluded that "the search for a new role definition and identity does not take the form of new professional ventures...
but rather of switching to another career which presumably offers greater
opportunities and power" (p. 331). A similar pattern has been described
in social work. Specht (1972) predicted, for instance, that as many social
work functions are taken on by non-MSWs, the field's higher status functions will be absorbed into other disciplines. At the same time, social
workers who perform administrative and planning roles in the field will
develop a new occupation. Based on this he concluded that social work
"will diminish in stature and become a *subprofessional* service" (p. 150).

The same phenomenon is evident in librarianship. With automation,
the field's already low status will decline even further as more and more of
its formerly professional tasks are performed by paraprofessionals and
clerical workers. At the same time, the few remaining higher status activities within the field are being renamed. Through this process, librarianship's identity as a low-status, female-intensive occupation can be escaped
by those who practice the "new" higher status functions. Thus, librarians
who wish to claim a status greater than that which librarianship affords
them may do so simply by renaming activities that were formerly part of
this occupation.

To witness this unfolding one need only look at the turf wars currently
being waged between academic librarians and their counterparts in university computing centers. As Veaner (1985) pointed out, "libraries and
computer centers have long been in competition for the same dollars.
Technology has advanced to the point where it is obvious that the two
agencies represent different faces of the same coin" (p. 227). However,

> while libraries seek to provide coherent access to information regardless of
> form, computer centers seek new territory to compensate for the demise of
> mainframe computing and shifting patterns of use. The mergers of library
> and computing centers are seen as a logical way to address the problem of
> boundaries. Few organizations, however, have successfully carried out a
> merger. In fact, mergers raise new issues about the professional role of the
> librarian. (Estabrook, 1989, p. 294)

And, of course, it is not only academic libraries that are being reshaped. In Britain, for instance, "public libraries are placed under the control of omnibus departments without a qualified librarian at the head" ("How the staff battled for chief's rights," 1977, p. 185). Similarly, special libraries are more and more likely to be "adopted by new parents—patents departments, management services departments, 'administration' and planning departments" (Lewis, 1980, p. 68).

As Cimbala observed, the main difference between the way in which libraries and university computing centers use computing is that,

> with the exception of functional activities, the library's electronic services largely reflect access to externally generated information, while computing centers are concerned primarily with internally produced data. (Cimbala, 1987, p. 394)

To eliminate any duplication in computing services within universities, Cimbala (Ibid.) suggested that what is needed is the development of scholarly information centers. The function of such centers, she argued, would be to assist patrons in gaining access to information (both print and machine-readable). Furthermore, they would be responsible for preparing data for input, purchasing systems, documents, hardware, software, and other media, as well as maintaining communications networks. However, she acknowledged that one impediment to bringing about such an integration of services is that few computing center staff (mostly men) would want to be labeled as librarians. Given this reluctance, it is probably not surprising that in the recent merger between the Stanford University Libraries and the university's Office of Information Resources, it was an engineer rather than the chief librarian who was placed in charge as "vice president for libraries and information resources" ("Budget struck Stanford library merged with computer center," 1990, p. 830)

In the face of such mergers and organizational reshuffling librarians have to wonder what the future will bring. For instance, will the freeing-up of professional librarians from the routinized functions of cataloging, reference, and collections really lead to the increase in user services that authors such as Buckland (1989) and Markuson (1976) have predicted? Perhaps. However, it is worth keeping in mind that

> when users gain access to information resources through remote systems, their relationships with library professionals and with the physical collection begin to change. These developments may enhance clients' regard for academic librarians if (1) users recognize the complexities of retrieving information from these new systems and (2) librarians' professional expertise is employed in systems development. (Estabrook, 1989, p. 290)

The issue of visibility was also raised by Veaner (1985) who noted that "the development of the so-called electronic library in higher education will impose even greater demands on academic librarians for, the less visible the medium, the greater the need for the intermediary" (p. 228).

On the other hand, Estabrook (1989) also noted that "it is equally likely that developments to increase the quality of end-user searching may reduce use (and therefore the perceived value) of the professional intermediary" (p. 290). Furthermore, she suggested, as services are increasingly located away from the library, "the relationship between the library and information delivery may be even less clear to library users" (p. 293). Thus, the perennial problem of the public's lack of recognition of library work is exacerbated by automated systems as users are even less likely than before to understand librarians' roles and the domain of knowledge represented by this profession.

IMPORTING OUTSIDE EXPERTS INTO THE LIBRARY

Many occupations are staking out their turf in the production and distribution of information. Who is responsible for what is an increasingly confusing issue in the information field since

> a fundamental characteristic of information makes the field especially difficult to delimit: information is everybody's business. It is a do-it-yourself field in which everyone has some interest and everyone has some competence. (Wilson, 1982, p. 181)

Thus, it is difficult to distinguish one type of information worker from another and to decide "what sort of recognition should be given for their performance" (Ibid., p. 182).

To complicate matters, not only are more and more people with diverse backgrounds describing themselves as information workers, but as noted in an earlier chapter, at the same time libraries are employing increasing numbers of people in senior positions who are not librarians. In particular, there has been a tendency to import managers and systems analysts who are, as Estabrook (1989) put it, "people with professional expertise vital to the library's growth but not necessarily related to the knowledge base of the profession" (p. 294). Vagianos and Lesser (1988) explained this trend with the claim that most librarians simply do not have the skills required to do their jobs. They argued that what is needed in librarianship is the ability "to handle the increasing complexity of the information environment and its increasing technological bias," but that

> this description does not fit enough professional librarians; nor does it reflect the professional training bias of many of the nation's library schools. (p. 15)

Applying similar reasoning, Cimbala (1987) suggested that in order to staff departments which represent the combination of university computing centers and libraries, what is needed is a "a hybrid librarian-computer scientist" (p. 396). In order to develop this hybrid, she urged library schools to "keep abreast of technological trends and still provide their students with a strong service orientation *and a bibliographic base*" (Ibid.; emphasis mine). Yet, as noted earlier, some of the schools, perhaps in their haste to appear technologically "fit," have removed cataloging courses as requirements in their programs (thereby effectively eliminating this bibliographic base). Other schools have developed special information science streams for their graduates; however, there is some question as to the value that is placed on teaching students about bibliographic control in these types of programs.

The demand for enhanced technological skills is not the only force that has resulted in the importing of outside experts into the library. There has also been a tendency to look externally for administrators. According to Winter (1988), when an occupation becomes increasingly specialized,

> administrators, once recruited informally from the ranks of practitioners, tend to be drawn into a separate pattern of professional development, with contrasting paths of entry, advancement and separation. (p. 90)

In librarianship the notion of administrative specialization is reflected in comments like those of Horn (1975) who argued that "library administration must be recognized as a profession in itself" (p. 471). In fact, McDermott (1984) observed that

> the fact that so many librarians pursue an MBA or MPA in order to prepare themselves for the most highly paid positions in the field is an indication that a different body of professional skills is needed for these positions, and that a manager's position may be correctly classified against criteria different from those applied to a 'worker's' position—be that worker professional or nonprofessional. (p. 21)

One outcome of this trend is the tendency within agencies, such as hospitals or libraries, to look increasingly for "professional managers," even though they may have no particular expertise or background within the particular professions over which they are in control. For example, in a controversial move, the board of the Enoch Pratt Free Library in Baltimore planned to hire a corporate executive (a man) as the chief executive officer, leaving the library director (a woman) in her job but reporting to the new CEO. However, before they could implement this plan the members of the board were informed that it would be in violation of Maryland's legal requirement "that all library systems be headed by certified librarians" ("Board's plan to hire CEO for Enoch Pratt draws fire," 1990,

p. 278). It is interesting to note, however, that a similar legal requirement was been eliminated in the province of Ontario when its Public Libraries Act was amended in 1984. Under the new Act, persons who are appointed as chief executive officers of public libraries are no longer required to hold a professional degree in librarianship. This amendment was vigorously opposed by many members of the library community, but to no avail.

One outcome of the separation between administrative and other streams of work in libraries is that it results in less of the work carried out in libraries being undertaken by "professional" librarians. According to Edwards (1975), administrators fail "to take professional functions sufficiently into account" (p. 158) and that when they attempt to save money by substituting paraprofessionals and clerical workers for professional librarians,

> a larger percentage of the time of librarians is devoted to managerial, especially supervisory, functions, and little or no additional time is devoted to professional functions—the functions for which the organization exists. (p. 158)

At the same time, then, that the professional library work force is declining through the deskilling effects of automation and government policy on employee classification, some of the most stable and lucrative positions in the field are being filled by people other than librarians. In academic libraries, for instance, Estabrook (1989) noted that

> whether it is because individuals outside the profession are thought to appear more sophisticated when dealing with the rich and famous or whether librarians are not credited with being aggressive enough for the current academic arena, a battle about the importance of professional education for professional positions, thought to have been won several decades ago, has reemerged as the nature of the work has changed. (p. 290)

In the coming decade, Veaner (1985) predicted that "all production aspects of ordering, receiving, checking in, and cataloging should be off-loaded to support staff, with a few librarians (or very senior support staff) to manage those operations" (p. 223). Somewhat optimistically he envisioned that the resulting "dramatic shift in staffing. . . does not mean any net reduction in total library staffing, but rather a reallocation of existing human resources" (p. 223). This scenario is doubtful at best. Instead, what is more likely to happen is that as nonprofessional staff take over routine functions, fewer professional librarians will be hired, especially with the ubiquitous increase in budgetary pressures (consider, for example, the financial difficulties which have arisen due to massive budget cuts in systems, such as the San Diego public library; "San Diego PL faces layoffs, possible 62% budget cut," 1990, p. 398).

Increasingly, M.L.S.-level librarians may be seen as an expensive luxury by fiscally minded administrators, particularly since less-educated staff can be brought in from library technician programs, for example, or from undergraduate programs in librarianship that will duplicate the B.S.W. type of preparation found in social work. This is already in evidence in Canada where there are at least two undergraduate programs in librarianship.

Although the provincial governments that support these programs have been subjected to considerable pressure from the library associations to withdraw their funding, their very development is indicative of the perceived market for "cheap" librarians.

INFORMATION AS A COMMODITY

Since the 1960s the sale of information and related products has become a booming business. As a result, the number of groups interested in the control of information has swelled considerably. In 1969 the Information Industry Association was formed in the United States "to promote private enterprise in the information field" (Crickman, 1979, p. 316). However, as Markuson (1976) noted, during the mid-1970s, although there was

> a reasonably good working relationship among the increasing number of players in the bibliographic control game. . . as this era draws to a close some of these people are becoming increasing strident. Complex issues have surfaced, such as copyright, data base ownership and access, the roles of public versus private sectors, etc. (p. 321)

Fifteen years later, these issues of territoriality and control of the information field are still contentious. Furthermore, there is an increasing recognition that money is to be made in the commodification of information. As White (1990) put it,

> libraries always stressed the value of information as a warm and fuzzy quality without defining it, but the new advocates are talking about information as return on investment and as a profitable commodity for a community seeking industrial development. (p. 265)

In the United States, information work is rapidly becoming privatized and is increasingly undertaken for exchange on the market. A decade ago, Estabrook (1981b) observed that

> it does not necessarily follow. . .that as information becomes more important, those organizations and professionals traditionally involved in the dis-

semination of information (for example, libraries and librarians) will assume a more important role. (p. 1377)

In fact, she predicted that "as information becomes more important, the owners of capital will appropriate the information utilities more directly for their purposes" (Ibid.). Time has proven her right. "While information work is a major responsibility of the public sector, the bulk of such work is done in the private sector, and the proportion done privately is increasing" (Kraft, 1987, p. 185). Furthermore, not only is the "work of distributing knowledge" *not* growing, but in the case of library workers, it is actually shrinking.

What is growing, however, is the number of private information services, that is, "those professionals who provide information relevant to the needs of individuals or firms" for profit (Ibid., p. 191). For instance, O'Leary (1987) noted that "the number of people with backgrounds as librarians or online searchers who are practicing independently has multiplied ten or twentyfold over the past 15 years" (p. 24). These individuals normally work as information brokers who offer "a for-profit version of traditional library reference service" or as information consultants "who tell you what to do with information and how to do it" (Ibid., p. 25).

In the early 1980s, Estabrook (1981b) also pointed out the value of libraries as marketing agents for information vendors.

> Libraries provide a limited but nonetheless important outlet for the sales of various types of technological and computer hardware and software. The adoption of these technologies by libraries is important not only for the profits that come to industry from their immediate purchase, but also because library use of such things as online data base searching prepares new markets for the information industry. (p. 1379)

Again, she was prophetic. According to Janke and Nicholls (in press), in the 1990s

> CD-ROM systems, externally leased and locally-subscribed databases, other emerging optical media, and ongoing developments in local database technology will continue apace. . . All these are enabling technologies, which place direct control of information resources of all types in the hands of the library user, where they belong. Just as the microcomputer inevitably eroded centralized computer services, including remote access to major databanks, in the 1980s; likewise, . . . the convergence of enabling technologies holds great promise for the decentralization of a wide range of library reference services in high-volume information seeking environments. (p. 12)

In other words, through the exposure received by these technologies in libraries, it seems that the vendors have indeed succeeded in creating an "end-user"market for their products. As this trend shows no signs of abating, one must again ponder the fate of libraries.

As libraries are increasingly automated or integrated into general departments of information or combined computing/library resource centers, the key issue facing librarians is who will be in control of what was formerly their territory. With the use of automated systems and reliance on utilities external to the library itself, the operation of academic libraries "become(s) increasingly bound up with the operations of campus and/or state systems" (Estabrook, 1989, p. 290). Complicating these issues of control is the fact that, with information being viewed more and more as a commodity, its price is rising. As a result, it costs more to run the library and, according to Vagianos and Lesser (1988), the "rising costs of materials in libraries in conjunction with their proliferation have seriously impaired the ability of libraries to maintain comprehensive collections" (p. 13). These pressures have forced many libraries to introduce user fees in order to cover costs, thereby compromising their mission to ensure universal access and bringing them into direct competition with the vendors.

> Libraries typically are publicly subsidized institutions. To mount their own electronic services in direct competition with private vendors makes them subject to charges of cross-subsidization and unfair competition. Worse still, to price library services at going market rates makes the library indistinguishable from the private vendors and disenfranchises that (significant) part of the library user constituency that cannot afford to pay the going market rate. (p. 14)

The uncertainty surrounding the role of libraries in the information field means a bewildering future for librarians. However, they are not the only occupational group whose status is unclear. Nurses, too, must sort out their roles in the face of the commodification of health care services. Particularly in the United States, "the notion of competition in health care is based on a free-market model that views health services as commodities which can be allocated by individual decisions in the marketplace" (Hash, 1982, p. 3). In the face of this competition, Hash (Ibid.) noted that there has been a rapid growth in the development of alternative health care delivery systems with "the consolidation and integration of hospitals into for-profit and not-for-profit chains; and in the emergence of new, specialized delivery mechanisms, such as surgi-centers, birthing centers, alcoholism treatment centers and the like" (p. 5). Thus, like librarians, nurses are finding their field in a profound state of flux in which their roles are altering significantly. Just as leaders in librarianship have urged their colleagues to take a proactive stance in relation to these changes, Hash (Ibid.) argued that "if nursing is to take advantage of this changing environment, it must recognize the opportunities to increase its visibility" (p. 4).

OVERVIEW

The introduction of automated systems in libraries has had, and will continue to have, an enormous impact on the composition and distribution of labor in the library workforce. Not only is it resulting in the deprofessionalizing of the core functions of librarianship (cataloging, collections development, and reference), as well as in the import of outside experts into key positions in the field, but it is also leading to a serious confrontation between libraries and that growing portion of the private sector concerned with the sale of information.

Despite the optimistic forecasts of high technology enthusiasts, it seems inevitable that the professional library workforce will continue to shrink and that the jobs remaining to librarians will be of a very different nature than those of the past. Many of the service roles played by librarians in the past will, in future, be taken over by paraprofessionals and clerical workers. This will leave the librarians to perform administrative and systems functions, both of which, coincidentally, are the highest status (and male-dominated) subfields within the profession. Paradoxically, however, it is these very subfields that are most threatened by the import of external expertise. Librarians are apparently not seen to be capable of grasping technological complexities nor are they perceived to be up to the job of managing the organization, whether it be in the form of a traditional library or an amalgam of "information services."

It appears, then, that librarianship is in the process of developing into a male field insofar as what is being emphasized, preserved, and valued in this occupation are those aspects which are administrative and technical and removed from direct contact with patrons. The irony in this is that, according to Toren (1975), the loss of the service ideal and loss of control over a knowledge base through the routinization of professional functions will lead to deprofessionalization. In other words, the changes underway in librarianship are likely to lead to its demise as a profession.

As this scenario unfolds what will happen to professional librarians, of whom the vast majority are women? Will the new information industry offer them an attractive alternative to employment in libraries? In the United States there has been a considerable increase in the number of women who have attained management positions in information work. However, according to Kraft (1987), "much of the increase of women in management does not represent real access to control for women" (p. 201). Instead, planning and control functions in the information field continue to be the purview of men. As Carter and Carter (1981) observed,

> there is a rapidly developing split in professional work between prestige jobs with good pay, autonomy, and opportunities for growth and development and a new class of more routinized, poorly paid jobs with little autonomy

and which are unconnected by promotion ladders to prestige jobs in the professions. . . . it is precisely in the newer, more routinized sector of professional employment that women's employment will be overwhelmingly concentrated. The upper tier of relatively autonomous work will continue to be male dominated with only token increases in female employment. Thus women's entry into the professions should be seen as something of a hollow victory: women will make gains, but the 'professional' jobs they enter will be such in name only. (p. 478)

One of the ironies for librarians in all of this is that there is now starting to be some recognition that in routinizing or deprofessionalizing the core functions of librarianship, the quality of the work being done in the field has been compromised. To cite just one example, it appears that a few people (other than catalogers themselves) are beginning to recognize that bibliographic control is threatened when databases are constructed and managed without input from cataloging experts. It seems, then, that the traditional skills of the profession may be valued once again. Unfortunately, their value is seen only in the face of a crisis. The question this raises, of course, is whether it is too late to save these aspects of librarianship or whether the pressures which result in deskilling will eliminate the profession entirely.

CHAPTER 8

Information for Sale: Profit Versus Public Good— What Happened to the Librarians?

Just as nurses find that they are, for the most part, excluded from the important policy decisions taken in the health care field, librarians, too, are largely ignored in the debate over the ownership of information. Traditionally, they have taken the stance that access to information should be available to all, regardless of ability to pay. However, as Schiller (1981) noted, "the social imperatives of information access are beginning to take second place to proprietary interests" (p. 708). Indeed, one finds an increasing concentration of control over information as its production and distribution rest in the hands of fewer and fewer players, of whom few, if any, are librarians.

According to Crickman (1979), there are three competing sectors in the information industry through which information products and services are offered to the market: private companies, nonprofit organizations, such as academic societies (for example, the American Chemical Society), and government agencies. Not surprisingly, these sectors are often at odds with one another

over which organizations should provide which services and products. Private companies are accused of profiting from information that was gathered or created at public expense, such as funded scientific research or census and economic indicator information. If such information must be sold, some maintain, it should be sold at the lowest possible price. (p. 316)

Private companies, on the other hand, argue that "government and not-for-profit organizations should reserve their productivity for those information products which the private sector cannot economically produce" (p. 317).

Throughout this debate, what is most important to recognize is "the increasing proprietary interest in information as a profitable resource as opposed to the diminishing concern for the social interest in information as a shared resource" (Schiller, 1981, p. 707). Librarians, with their emphasis on equity of access, have raised the ire of private sector advocates who claim that they are "demeaning the value of the information they provide by not making the public aware of the. . . cost of its provision" (Crickman, 1979, p. 317). One observer noted, for instance, that the information industry has always had to fight the so-called "Carnegie Syndrome," that is, the idea that information should be free and the resulting tendency for people not to put any value on it (O'Leary, 1987, p. 28). Ironically, however, as Crickman (1979) and many others have pointed out, advocates of the information "industry," especially information brokers, often depend on publicly funded libraries in order to locate the very information for which they later extend a charge to their clients.

The tug-of-war between private and public interests in the information sector is often played out in courts of law. Recently, for instance, the giant database vendor Dialog Information Services initiated a lawsuit against the American Chemical Society. The A.C.S., which makes its database accessible through the Chemical Abstracts Service, competes with Dialog, which also sells access to parts of this database. The basis for Dialog's suit against the A.C.S. is that the Society's not-for-profit status makes it an unfair competitor. Dialog claims that the Chemical Abstracts Service "is a government-subsidized operation, since it developed its database with the aid of over $15 million in National Science Foundation funding" ("Dialog sues Chemical Abstracts charging antitrust violations," 1990, p. 625).[1]

Such disputes are not uncommon and it is clear that not only are the private business interests in the information sector winning a good number of them, but that these interests are increasingly concentrated. At present, for example, transnational corporations not only control much of the publishing industry, but only "five companies control 90% of data-

---

[1] It is interesting that in such disputes over proprietary rights to information, the most significant protagonists often have had nothing to do with the creation of the information they are selling. For instance, Haar (1986) pointed out that the big companies marketing online retrieval systems "do not create their own databases; rather they buy databases, mostly indexing and abstracting services, from producers" (p. 40) and then sell access to this information to librarians and others. In other words, he noted, "most of the business in the field is done by the 'wholesalers' who act as middlemen between database creators and users" (Ibid.).

base sales" ("How crucial leadership is—who are we; what we do," 1990, p. 689).

VALUE CLASHES IN THE INFORMATION SECTOR

According to Webster and Robins (1986), the "information revolution has little to do with making information into a generally available resource; it has everything to do with turning it into a profitable industry" (p. 329). Furthermore, they observed,

> the current wave of commercialization and privatization of those information and communications media that support what remains of the public sphere threatens to subvert the possibility of informed public reasoning and exchange of ideas. It offers the prospect of communication giving way to more industrialized consumption on an ability to pay basis. (p. 330)

In Britain, for example, government information services are being increasingly privatized, as are government computer operations, developments which, Webster and Robins (Ibid.) claim, "threaten to bring social data and statistics into the private sphere, where they are subject to commercial imperatives" (p. 331).

Citizen access to government information is also diminishing in the United States through the accelerating movement to privatize public information (Heanue, 1988), the awarding of federal contracts to outside information organizations (Schiller, 1981), as well as through the reduction in the number of government documents printed, and the lack of compliance with the Freedom of Information Act on the part of government agencies (Gray, 1987). Unfortunately, attempts to regulate the distribution of government information and preserve a meaningful system of access through the development of a coherent and enforceable information policy have been sporadic and piece-meal. Gray noted, for example, that in many instances no provision for free public access to information is made once government information is transferred to the private sector, and that "no legislative action has tied together the laws and regulations regarding the print, communications, and electronic media" (p. 7).

The U.S. National Commission on Library and Information Science (N.C.L.I.S.), the agency which is supposed to advise the government on national library and information policy and which should, in fact, provide this coordinating function, is in difficulty because of underfunding (see, for example, Hernon and McClure, 1987), lack of clarity in its mandate, and commissioners who have alienated the library community. It has come under a great deal of criticism, for instance, as a result of its apparent support of the F.B.I.'s controversial "Library Awareness Program" —a bizarre plan to encourage library workers to alert the Bureau about individuals (presumably spies) who show an interest in reading "suspicious" technical materials. Even the N.C.L.I.S. membership is problematic due to an uneven split between those with entrepreneurial interests in the information sector and others who are more concerned with public access.

PUBLIC ACCESS

The very administration of federal government information is problematic with respect to public access. The U.S. Office of Management and Budget (O.M.B.) has sweeping powers in the management of federal information; however, its focus is "limited to controlling government costs, internal operations, and the use of information technology" (McClure, Bishop, and Doty, 1989, p. 55). Users of information, especially those external to the administration of the federal government, "receive little attention in O.M.B. policy statements" (Ibid., p. 56). Indeed, McClure, Bishop and Doty (Ibid.) suggest that the O.M.B. has done little to increase access to government information and may be doing "more harm than good" (p. 59).

With the O.M.B.'s apparent fixation on efficiency and information technology, it is perhaps not surprising that a preponderance of its "information resource managers" come from data processing backgrounds. Their influence has resulted in a "technical perspective...[which] ignores user information needs and effective dissemination of agency information" (Ibid.). Furthermore, there are indications that these managers tend to view information activities that are externally focused, that is, focused on public users, such as those offered by libraries, "as 'janitorial services'" (Ibid.).[2]

As part of its role in providing public access to government information, the U.S. Federal government does operate several depository programs including that of the Government Printing Office (G.P.O.) through which

> member libraries...are expected 'to make depository publications available for the free use of the general public' and to answer reference questions or make referral to a source that will answer the questions. (Hernon and McClure, 1987, p. 11)

However, according to Hernon and McClure, not only is there "minimal coordination" (Ibid., p. 287) among the various depository programs, but

---

[2] The attitude of these managers reflect, once again, a general disdain for the values and activities of librarianship, even within the so-called "information sector."

the G.P.O. program has not been adequately funded, does a poor job of using modern information retrieval procedures, and provides "minimal training and support for assisting users in accessing technologically based information" (Ibid., p. 192). Furthermore, consistent with Gray's (1987) observation above, although all government publications are to be made available to depository libraries, "many agencies successfully ignore the program and do not distribute their publications through it" (Hernon and McClure, 1987, p. 288). In other words, in spite of the mechanisms which exist, presumably, to guarantee public access to information, various sectors within the U.S. Federal government seem, often, to be at cross purposes with the result that access is in jeopardy.

The Role of Public Libraries

Only a relatively small percentage of the libraries which participate in the U.S. Federal government's depository program are public libraries (Hernon and McClure, 1988). However, since they are charged with the mandate to make information available to members of the public, regardless of their ability to pay, one would expect public libraries to play an increasingly prominent role in the face of the growing commercialization in the information sector. Unfortunately, however, this does not seem to be the case. If anything, the reverse seems to be true. Access to information through public libraries in Britain, Canada, and the United States is severely threatened by underfinancing. In 1991, for example, the New York Public Library faced budget cuts for the third consecutive year, while in Britain libraries have been told to "look beyond the traditional sources of funds and to consider whether some costs may be recovered from users" (Webster and Robins, 1986, p. 331). Similar pressures to raise funds are also being placed on American and Canadian librarians. As a result, more and more public librarians are having to turn their hands to fundraising, in some cases to generate operating funds, not just to raise money for capital projects (see, for example, Berry, 1986). This is, of course, completely at odds with the notion that public libraries (i.e., publicly funded libraries providing public access) should carry the brunt of the responsibility for ensuring the equitable distribution of information across the community.

INFORMATION TECHNOLOGY

At the very heart of the dispute over private versus public ownership of information are the new information technologies which, according to Buschman (1990), are redefining copyright and putting public access on shaky ground. CD-ROM products are being produced and marketed to maintain the overall profits of producers—not to maximize access. Trade groups like the Information Industry Association lobby Congress for higher fees and for shifting more government information to private database vendors. (p. 1026)

Making an argument similar to that of Webster and Robins (1986), Buschman (1990) pointed out that

> information technology has made possible the selling-off of government information to private vendors and the general policy of treating that information as a commodity. In the process, access to this privatized information, collected at taxpayer's expense, has been restricted. (p. 1027)

It would seem then that the most important implication of both information technology and profit seeking in the information sector is the threat they both pose to public access. Indeed, Caudle and Levitan (1989) reported that within the U.S. Federal government,

> increasing shifts to electronic dissemination systems... tended to restrict dissemination of public information [and]...[government] agencies have not reformulated policy on the dissemination of public information to realign the impact of information technology with traditional values concerning public information dissemination. (p. 300)

Furthermore, Hernon and McClure (1987) pointed out that, despite the significant commitment of funds to the purchase and development of information technology, "existing Federal policies related to the use, application, and public access to that information is unclear, contradictory, and oftentimes, non-existent" (p. 190).

In the 1970s, Wessel (1976) observed that "information, power, and wealth are inextricably linked. The wise, the powerful, and the wealthy have not always taken kindly to the idea of letting the public freely browse about in their domains" (p. 62). Because of their generally poor status and lack of visibility, librarians, and traditional guardians of democratic access, are poorly placed to fend off the forces that mitigate against access for, as Estabrook (1981b) so astutely observed,

> it does not necessarily follow... that, as information becomes more important, those organizations and professionals traditionally involved in the dissemination of information (for example, libraries and librarians) will assume a more important societal role. Nor does it follow that ownership of capital will be replaced by ownership of knowledge as the basis for societal power. Rather, it can be argued that, as information becomes more important, the owners of capital will appropriate the information utilities more directly for their purposes. (p. 1377)

Developing an argument based on Luddism, Webster and Robins (1986) took the position that developments in information technology "must be regarded as inherently social and therefore a result of values and choices" rather than as "unstoppable and unobjectionable," "asocial and neutral" (p. 4). When one examines the social implications of information technology it is essential to look beyond the mere storage and retrieval capacities of the technology. In other words, despite the fact that computerized information retrieval systems have tremendous capabilities in the management of information, a much more important feature of these systems is their potential for information control.

> The importance and power of computers lie not merely in increased capabilities to handle vast amounts of information. Of more concern is the potential computers offer to process and transform such information masses more in accordance with our various needs. . . . It is precisely these. . . capabilities to process, manipulate, combine and arrange information offered by computerized information retrieval systems, to make information far more useful by its transformation into forms and arrangements that better match needs, to which the questions of public access must be addressed. And to the extent that ownership of such systems implies the control of access to these capabilities, then it is the ownership of information retrieval systems that is of far more concern than the ownership of such information per se. (Wessel, 1976, p. 63)

With the advent of these new technologies, the ability of librarians to control information has been dramatically altered and eroded. As De Gennaro (1989) pointed out, 20 years ago libraries were the "the sole or primary source of interlibrary loan or document supply" (p. 43). However, this function is now being taken over by other information vendors. And, even though "the market demand for documents has increased enormously in the last 20 years, and while the number of library transactions is increasing, the market share of the new vendors is increasing far more rapidly" (p. 43). In other words, relative to the private sellers of information, librarians are losing ground in the "free" or public provision of information.

In addition to the shift which has taken place in the types of demands being placed on libraries, the relationship between libraries and the very sources of information upon which they rely are changing as well. In some instances librarians are no longer purchasing information sources which can then be used at will. Rather, the library's position vis-à-vis many reference sources is becoming, essentially, that of a lessee, that is, a non-owner paying for temporary access. The online retrieval industry, then, limits the public availability of information

> by retaining ownership of the databases involved and merely provides customer librarians with temporary and limited access to them. This is a

critical departure from the traditional mode, in which libraries purchase databases (indexes, abstracts, books, or whatever) directly from vendors or publishers and can therefore provide public access to the data (i.e., information) as they wish. . . . the industry has fostered restrictive access to information on the basis of cost. Because online systems are expensive, most libraries pass part of their cost on to the partron in the form of search fees. This effectively diminishes or even denies the opportunity to acquire information to those who cannot afford the charges. (Haar, 1986, p. 41)

PAYING FOR INFORMATION

For most public librarians, the notion of "fee for service" is anathema. In fact, in 1977 the American Library Association Council "branded levying fees for information as discriminatory and staunchly advocated equal access to information in principle" (Haar, 1986, p. 41). However, as Haar (Ibid.) pointed out, while this may be a widely held principle, what is actually practiced in libraries at present "is quite another matter; charging for online retrieval appears to remain much more the rule than the exception among libraries" (p. 41). The implications of fee charging are extensive. Govan (1988) argued, for instance, that

> to the degree that libraries become retailing shops, to that degree will librarians cease to be professionals and will become shopkeepers, of necessity. Among the many qualities lost will be service to unprofitable 'markets,'. . . and acquisition of seldom-used materials. (p. 38)

Beginning in the 1960s with the sale of photocopies, libraries, according to De Gennaro (1989), "have been compelled to begin selling certain high-tech services to their users" (p. 42). As a result of the increasing integration of a variety of information technologies into most libraries of any size, by now "the fight to make the burgeoning new computer technology available without fees has by and large been lost" (Blake, 1988, p. 12). At present, then, Blake (1988) claims that "most libraries deny access to computerized information to those without the money to pay" (p. 12).

Some librarians have embraced the introduction of fees with enthusiasm, seeing them as an important source of revenue and even, perhaps, as a means of enchancing the public's respect for librarianship. The latter view is based on the assumption that people assign greater value and prestige to that for which they have to pay. Obviously, these librarians have the idea that if information and services related to its provision are clearly seen to come at a price, librarians will, correspondingly, rise in the public's estimation. Govan (1988), however, disagreed with this notion, suggesting instead that the new enthusiasm for entrepreneurship in libraries is ill-founded. The market is not sufficiently large nor the products sufficiently valued to create income equal to the loss of public support for libraries that fees for service will prompt. (p. 38)

Also, as mentioned in the previous chapter, librarians who embrace the new technologies and charge for information services may eventually put themselves out of business. By making the new systems available they are performing what amounts to a marketing function for the vendors. In other words, libraries are basically operating as test markets for new information products. When a segment of the public is hooked, interested consumers can bypass the library and purchase the product or service directly from the vendor (if they can afford it).

Also related to the question of fees is that of quality of service. According to Govan (Ibid.), "one of the most distressing aspects of the support for entrepreneurial librarianship is its relative indifference to service" (p. 38). He argued that

the concept of brokering commodities as opposed to rendering services implies an entirely different atmosphere for librarians, one in which fees for service... not only became acceptable, but in which income replaces satisfied patrons as the overriding goal. Furthermore, the patron, transformed into a paying customer, will assume different attitudes and values as well, and any semblance of common purpose between librarian and library user will fade significantly. (p. 38)

Clearly then the charging of user fees in libraries is only one aspect of a much broader issue with respect to maintaining public access to information. As Bearman (1987) noted, what is more significant than the question of fees "is the fact that we are witnessing a serious questioning of our fundamental notion of public good, as debates rage over the responsibilities of the government to provide information to its citizenry" (p. 85).

UNEQUAL ACCESS

One disturbing trend resulting from the many changes wrought by the information technologies is a growing information classism which has the potential to cause great rifts in the community. According to Smith (1989),

if libraries and librarians fail to play an active role in the 'information economy' by embracing the new conduits of information, other players such as information brokers will fill the gap—at a price—and thus serve to further polarize society into two classes: the information rich and the information poor. (p. 34)

Of course, there have always been information "haves" and "have nots," that is, people with varying degrees of awareness about, and access to, the record of human knowledge. Childers (1975) observed, for instance, that

> all people need essentially the same kind of information to survive in this society, but the disadvantaged individual needs large remedial doses of information in order to bring him (sic) up to 'information par' with the rest of society. (p. 35)

In order to even up the score, public libraries have existed in North America since the 1800s as a (potentially) equalizing force. While it is debatable whether they have been effective in this respect, the very existence of such an institution is significant for it indicates a long-standing recognition that access to information is every citizen's right, and that an informed populace is an important component of a well-functioning democracy. On the other hand,

> the current wave of commercialization and privatization of those information and communications media that support what remains of the public sphere threatens to subvert the possibility of informed public reasoning and exchange of ideas. It offers the prospect of communication giving way to more individualized consumption on an ability to pay basis. (Webster and Robins, 1986, p. 330)

Webster and Robins (Ibid.) argued, in fact, that

> the deregulation and privatization of the information sector that is being promoted by both the British and American governments...amounts to an undermining of the status of knowledge as a 'social good', an assault on the public sphere. (p. 329)

Indeed, Hernon and McClure (1987) suggested that, at least in the United States, the federal government's methods of providing information to the public have resulted in a situation wherein

> it is communicating more with the information-rich, those able to pay for information and be both articulate and forceful in their information requests to Executive Branch officials and members of Congress. The government is definitely questioning its responsibility to provide information to the public free of charge. (p. 259)

Information with Low Income Potential

Another alarming possibility associated with the commodification of information is that when certain types of information are not highly saleable or are of primary interest to markets in which there is not a great deal of money available they may simply not be produced anymore. Recognizing this problem Vagianos and Lesser (1988) warned that

> if information cannot command a large enough market to make it commercially viable to offer, it may fail to be disseminated and, ultimately, to be produced. Information that is paid for is expected to have value for the buyer. Should this mean that the value of information is to be determined only by such a market criterion? Where price is concerned, who is being excluded on the basis of ability to pay, and what are the implications of such exclusion? (p. 14)

Blake (1988) raised similar questions about this issue, noting that charging fees for information changes the nature of information:

> The specific kinds of information poor people need are least likely to be collected for commercialized databases. . . . Who is interested in collecting and distributing up-to-date information about free child care services or free well-baby clinics or available free shelters or free hot meals? Those who need such information can't pay for it, so it ceases to exist. (p. 12)

As though to bear out Blake's prediction, one noteworthy victim of commercial market failure is the database, Catalyst Resources for Women, at one time available on BRS but which was dropped from this service in 1989.[3]

Serving the Marginal Client

It is probably not coincidental that public libraries, which are now under increasing financial pressure have, for many years, had women as their primary consumers. In fact, Hole (1990) chided librarians for "feminizing" the public libraries and making them "into institutions that are hostile or useless to most males" (p. 1076).[4] What she ignored in her argument, of course, is that most public institutions support male interests almost exclusively[5] and that women, whose income, on average, is approx-

---

[3] The Catalyst online database was created from a library collection developed by the Catalyst organization, a nonprofit group founded in the 1960s to address the concerns of women reentering the labor force (Barribeau, 1985). The library collection is focused primarily on issues affecting working women.

[4] Hole's (1990) contention is, of course, arguable. In my experience, public libraries are generally well stocked with many "male-centered" materials such as repair manuals for what seems to be to be an endless number of different makes of car.

[5] One need only consider, for example, the resources allocated in any community to sports activities. Facilities and funding are always considerably more generous for those interested in football and ice hockey than for sports and leisure activities that might be of greater interest to women.

imately 60 percent that of men's, are precisely the sorts of people who may need access to the commercially nonviable information described by Blake (1988).

So, what lies ahead for those who comprise the markets in which the commercial information vendors have no interest? The private sector response to this question is, of course, that the information needs of those who are not in the economic mainstream should be met through publicly supported institutions. However, while politicians and those with interests in the private sector may pay lip service to this idea, the very institutions that are supposed to provide this access are coming increasingly under attack through major cuts to their funding. As a result, the production and distribution of diverse types of information are severely jeopardized. A case in point is the recent history of the Canadian Broadcasting Corporation (C.B.C.) (Canada's public radio and television system). The C.B.C., which has been the target of massive funding cuts over the last few years, recently announced the layoffs of hundreds of employees and major cuts in regional programming at the same time that its service mandate was extended by the very government that slashed its budget.

User Sophistication

In the mid-1970s, Childers's (1975) view was that both the formal and informal channels of information transfer were "available to everyone in society, and everyone uses them both" (p. 38). Today, however, with the increasing complexity of information technologies, these assumptions about access may no longer be viable. At present, access to information does not simply vary depending on whether a person chooses to use one type of information source more than another. Instead, today's potential users must have considerable skill in order to gain access to many of the channels through which information might be passed, in addition to needing sufficient financial resources to pay for access to these channels. As Haar (1986) pointed out, "the irony in all this is that as more sophisticated tools are developed to access information, it well could become less accessible to more people" (p. 43). Thus, "some segments of society are already receiving more benefits from new technologies and information because they have both the sophistication to use them and the money to pay for them" (Schuman, 1982, p. 1061).

Observing that the pressure to be efficient in libraries seems to be winning out over the desire to ensure access, Estabrook (1981b) commented that

reference questions that can be answered efficiently are preferred over ones that are too complex, too vague, too 'off-the-wall'! Problems that take too much staff time are referred to other organizations. And increasingly it appears that services will be targeted to those clients known to be the library's most likely customers and to those who can pay (if not in money, then in community influence and power). The middle-class patterns of service in libraries are well documented. . . . there are a number of indications that libraries are giving up on attempts to serve those individuals who have not been or are not likely to be users. One might call this the triage effect. As pressures increase to make services productive, as resources are diminished, it becomes necessary to treat or serve those clients who will survive, not those who will probably fall by the wayside as clients. No effort is made to serve or treat them. Even as this is done, the options become more limited, for the information industry is rapidly moving to take over the library services that may be profitable for them. If these businesses continue to develop as they have, and gradually provide greater and more direct access to data bases and ready reference information, libraries are going to be pushed into a more limited societal role—something that will further affect their funding. (p. 1380)

Echoing many of Estabrook's observations are the findings in a recent study about access to birth control information in public libraries. Lundberg (1991) found that access to this information was restricted because librarians have little time to search for ephemeral materials such as pamphlets, publications from women's presses, and government documents (materials which tend, unfortunately, to constitute much of what is available on this subject), and because they have lost much of their professional autonomy as a result of the centralizing of acquisition and cataloging processes due, largely, to the introduction of automated systems.

FIGHTING BACK:
THE LIBRARIAN'S ROLE IN PRESERVING ACCESS

For Haar (1986), the issue of access "is no less than the open and democratic provision of information, one that cannot be irresponsibly sloughed off on the grounds of economic expediency" (p. 43). In fact, Buschman (1990) argued that as a result of the sweeping changes occurring in the production and dissemination of information because of the new technologies, "we run the risk of creating an information technocracy and an information elite" (p. 1030). Thus, librarians who are concerned with preserving access must raise their voices for, as Hernon and McClure (1988) asked (with respect to access to government information), "if documents librarians do not advocate and strive for improved services and access to government information who will?" (p. 482).

Recommending economic measures as a means by which to resist some of the concentration of control and the difficulties in access that are arising out of the activities of private interests in the information business, Haar (1986) suggested that, in order to guarantee access of information to ordinary users in the short run, librarians should "insist that producers of online databases also produce the same data in print. This would mean a refusal to buy the online version if no print version were available" (p. 43). In the long term, however, he recommended that libraries "form a nonprofit consortium to vend databases, a system that would assure them of control of the data and methods of access to it" (p. 43).

Recognizing the need to consider the changes that are occurring in the information sector due to the new technologies, some librarians have, indeed, begun to act. For instance, various committees have been established within the American Library Association to ponder such questions as the impact of technology on the production and dissemination of information, and the government's role in collecting and disseminating information. To date, however, it is not at all clear what kind of impact (if any) these efforts have had on the development of information policy in the United States.

Professionalism and Access to Information

In some respects, the ideology of professionalism is at odds with the ethic of equity in access. As noted in earlier chapters, one of the characteristics of traditional male professions, such as law, is that its members take on the role of the expert vis-à-vis the client, dispensing information for a fee. In the past, librarianship has offered an alternative to this model. Rather than operating as the expert dispenser, the librarian has assumed, instead, the role of intermediary—working to match the client's need to the information resources available. Within this type of relationship it is the client rather than the professional who decides what kinds of information she or he wishes to have, as well as how to use the information. At risk, then, when a female-intensive, service-oriented occupation, such as librarianship, is in search of a new, higher status identity is the loss of this relationship. In other words, the pursuit of professionalism may very well be incompatible with the equitable sharing of resources.

The threat posed to clients when the members of a field become preoccupied with professionalism has been noted in nursing as well. For instance, Partridge (1978) observed that value conflicts in nursing

> are painfully evident in our quest for professional status. Nursing identifies with the prestigious professions, attempting to pattern itself according to characteristics of a profession as elucidated by sociologists. The sad realities of professionalism in our day-to-day health care system, however, seem to conflict with the sociological concepts. Patients are afraid to ask questions and are bullied or ignored when they do. (p. 357)

Furthermore, not only does the expert model undermine the quality of the relationship between professional and patron, but it also favors the delivery of service to those who can afford to pay.

This perspective on professionalism is already evident in librarianship. For instance, Govan (1988) reported that "for the first time [librarians] are openly advocating the 'privatization' of [the] profession" (p. 36). These librarians have embraced the information industry, hoping to sell to their clients what was once provided as a free public service. Of course, the draw of the private sector is understandable since it offers the possibility of greater autonomy and income than might be available in an institutional setting. However, what is evident in all the female-intensive fields in which practitioners migrate to private practice is that it results in a fundamental shift in the nature of service. For instance, because of new licensure arrangements, social work practice need no longer take place within traditional service agencies (Blumenstein, 1988). Thus, many social workers now work full time as independent practitioners serving clients who can affort to pay their fees, leaving behind the less experienced workers in the agencies that provide services for the less privileged. Similarly, in what is becoming, essentially, the private practice of librarianship, one may see the activities of librarians cum "information brokers" resulting in much the same pattern. As Blanke (1989) argued, "the library profession's eagerness to be in the vanguard of a post-industrial information society may cause an erosion of its public service commitments in favor of a role as a servant to a technocratic elite" (p. 39).

Another feature of the pursuit of professionalism is that clients who hold some prestige in the community come to be seen as more desirable targets of service than those who are disadvantaged. Again, however, by focusing their attentions on higher status clients such as members of the business community, librarians may be working against their own interests. In making such a choice they play directly into the hands of those who claim that publicly supported libraries are in unfair competition with enterprises in the private sector which sell information for a profit.

Also symptomatic of the pull of professionalism in librarianship is the field's almost reckless embrace of technology. As Buschman (1990) observed, librarians have bought the hype surrounding information technology "in order to alter the profession's traditionally poor image and status" (p. 1026). However, as noted in the previous chapter, by taking the field in this direction librarians may very well put themselves out of business as more sophisticated users gain access directly to the sources of information they need, bypassing librarians entirely.[6] Furthermore, since the technology creates a fee-charging environment in the library, the users who are most likely to require the assistance of an intermediary are less and less likely to get it. Not only does the potential charge for information delivery

---

[6] Given the extreme pressure to integrate automated systems into nearly every organizational environment in the developed world, librarians are, of course, in a "Catch-22" situation since, in all likelihood, they would also be bypassed if they turned their backs on at least some aspects of this technology.

preclude use for some, it is also very likely that the type of information sought may no longer be available (either because it has not been compiled or because the form in which it is produced has made it inaccessible).

Accompanying the import of the new technologies into libraries are the technical experts who support them. These individuals, too, pose a threat to the traditional service ethic. Since they are not trained in librarianship, few computing experts can be expected to hold the same beliefs about equity in access to information as do their librarian colleagues. However, because the computing systems experts are viewed with some awe within the field they often wield considerable influence and they (along with the administrative experts who are also imported from outside the profession) have the potential to shift policy in directions other than those with which many librarians would be comfortable. Given the attitudes of the information resource managers in the O.M.B., for instance, policy shifts that might be fostered by these "foreigners" in libraries might be toward the broader acceptance of user fees or toward an emphasis on greater efficiency in service. In fact, this may already be happening. Blanke (1989) observed, for example, that "matters of technical innovation and efficiency are increasingly overriding equity of public service as library goals" (p. 40). The problem with such emphases, at least in public libraries, is that, as Smith (1989) reminded us, "efficiency is not equity and violates the main premise upon which public libraries are supported" (p. 34).

CONCLUSION

The technological developments of the last two decades have imposed an agenda on librarians that not all may be anxious to embrace. Clearly, issues of access, control over information resources, and even the very nature of work in the field must be of concern to all in the profession. Govan (1988) put it nicely when he noted that "the issue is one of professional values and priorities. Instead of entering the business world, librarians should turn their thoughts and energies to preserving the established values of their profession in the electronic age" (p. 38). However, this does not simply require a renewed commitment to the values of access and service. Rather, if librarians are to have any say in setting their national information policy agendas, they must be politically active for, as Blanke (1989) warned, if they refuse "to define their values in political terms and actively defend those values against the interests of wealth and power, such fundamental library ideals as free and equal access to information are in jeopardy" (p. 40).

CHAPTER 9

A Question of Values

By now it should be clear that the pressures reshaping the field of librarianship are tremendous. The extent to which librarians will be able to exercise any control over the field's evolution (or devolution) will be determined, largely, by the values they bring with them to this process.

According to Lewis (1977), when the female-intensive fields "offer rewards for displays of assertiveness and remove women from the direct control of males, these professions may provide conditions which nurture female autonomy" (p. 103). In other words, in spite of the poor wages and lack of esteem accorded to them, occupations such as librarianship and nursing have offered women a chance, historically, to develop work environments and methods of service delivery that are, at least to some degree, a reflection of themselves.

This view of the female-intensive professions illustrates the need for what Marshall (1989) called "a new theory of careers." Claiming that traditional career theory "is rooted in male values and based on disguised male psychology; it neglects or devalues the feminine" (p. 282), Marshall suggested that, as an alternative, we look again at the roles into which women have been socialized. "Instead of seeing these roles as of low social worth because that is how a patriarchal society defines them" (Ibid.), Marshall is of the opinion that we should attempt to reclaim the positive aspects of these roles.

What Marshall argued for is, essentially, a revaluing of women's work, a notion that has been embraced by a number of members of the female-intensive fields. As one nursing association leader put it, we need to rely on a feminist analysis to "teach us how to analyze and challenge power structures, both in society and in the health care system, and to value women's experience without reference to male standards" (Thomas, 1990, p. 14). Similarly, Partridge (1978) claimed that we have to stop abandoning our values as women and nurses. Based on a mis-diagnosis of what would give us power and status as professionals, we have set about taking on all the attributes of our male and 'fully professional' col-leagues in the traditional professions. . . . I believe it to be a disservice to our-selves, to health care, and to society to seek equality with the male on *his* terms in *his* society where *his* values predominate. (p. 357)

While Partridge's (Ibid.) remarks were aimed specifically at nurses, they apply equally well to the other female-intensive fields for, as Nelson (1980) pointed out,

the image of the professional is decidedly masculine. The professional is in authority, he commands respect, and he has control over a world of knowl-edge which the layman cannot enter. The librarian's image is feminine: will-ing to serve and anxious to give the client what he wants. In fact, the librarian is dedicated to making available to the lay public that knowledge which the professional is anxious to control. The professional keeps his client in a sub-servient position. The librarian respects his client by collecting information, making it available, and instructing the client in how to locate it; the client is assumed to have the intelligence to know what to do with it. (p. 2032)

Thus, rather than be concerned that librarianship is failing to exemplify the expert model of the male professions, librarians might do well to ponder Asheim's (1979) view that

the tendency to instruct patrons in skills by which they can help themselves instead of turning always to us, may be a desirable aspect of our social contri-butions that we do not wish to change. (p. 253)

What is really at issue here, then, is a question of what is valued in the female fields. As Welch (1980) put it, the "dangers of abandoning feminine values while attempting to develop masculine values. . . [are] loss of holistic approaches to practice and a diminution of the concept of caring" (p. 724).

Bernard (1981) described very clearly the conflict that faces women in the workplace and that is reflected in the opposing forces which affect the development of the female-intensive occupations:

Because the economic rewards are so much greater in the male world than in the female world, some women in the labor force reject the female world, they see it as an encumbrance to their own success in the male world; they want none of it. They want to discard their 'old country' ways, as successful immigrants did, and take on those of the 'new country.' They want to be 'assimilated.' Thus a considerable spate of books began to appear in the 1970s to teach women the rules of the game as played in the male world so that they would know how it operated and learn how to deal with it. The authors of one such book were, in fact, called 'missionaries to a female population that wants to be converted. (p. 221)

As Marshall (1989) pointed out, however, these tides may be turning as more and more women discover what is in store for them in this "male world:"

> Many women have become disillusioned with reform. Their participation in the world that men have shaped does little to counteract its basic devaluing of female characteristics. Women were offered opportunities to join men on their terms, men making little accommodation in return. Disillusion about the burden of having multiple roles. . . and adapting to organizational norms. hostile to more female ways of being. . . have led some women to moderate their work goals and others to question the demands organizations make on women and men. A more radical voice is re-emerging, seeking change in the structure and practices of employment. (p. 276)

The most important aspect of this change will mean learning how to appreciate women's work and women's values. As noted many times in the various chapters of this book, librarians, nurses, social workers, and others in the female-intensive fields offer the public an alternative to the male professions in which the expert knows best. In fact, what character-izes service delivery in all these fields, whether it involves information, health care, or family support, is that it not only gives over control to the client, but is widely available since it is much less expensive than the ser-vices normally offered through the male professions. This service alter-native may well be lost, however, if the members of the women's fields, in their pursuit of status, adopt the male model of professionalism, lose sight of their own values and, in so doing, betray their own traditions.

As the economy changes and the service sector expands there is an increasing privatization of the services which have been traditionally performed by members of the female-intensive professions who have, his-torically, been in the employ of public institutions. If we are to have any hope of slowing this transition and maintaining a meaningful level of equity in access, we must abandon any notions of professionalism that encourage political neutrality. Instead, it is time to realize that both the clients of the female-intensive professions and the workers in these fields have much to gain if their leaders recognize a common feminist agenda—that of acknowledging and rewarding work that has been traditionally done by women and fighting to preserve the values that are the under-pinnings of this work.

TOWARD A NEW LIBRARIANSHIP

If we are to embrace Marshall's "radical voice" we may find a new librarian-ship. "New," in this sense, means reconsidering and, perhaps, reembracing the old librarianship by restoring to it a brand of female professionalism.

This includes a (re)commitment to service (based on a female rather than a male model), advocacy vis-à-vis the public's right to equitable access to information; and activism with respect to employment issues including status, salary, and equity in the workplace. It comes down, in other words, to the members of the field embracing a feminist analysis of their profession.

In practical terms, librarians must take several steps if they wish to achieve these goals, regain control over their occupation, and stake a stronger claim to their portion of the information sector "turf." First, they must pressure the library associations to take an explicit and uncompromising employee-centered stance, even if it means a reduction in membership. Failure to recognize the inherent conflicts represented by membership rosters that include both employers and employees and which are institution-centered rather than employee-focused will result, inevitably, in an inability to generate and act on policies that will improve the status and salaries of the members of this profession.

Librarians must also work to ally themselves with those in other female-intensive professions and acknowledge that many of the externally imposed impediments to their goals are the result of the way in which female endeavor is valued in this culture. As mentioned several times previously, this means undertaking a feminist agenda for change in conjunction with other groups whose members have similar concerns.

Finally, librarians must give themselves credit for what they know and put a stop to the process of shunning the female-intensive aspects of their work. This means recognizing that attempts to relabel library work as something else, especially "information brokerage" or "information science" is, essentially, wrongheaded (and, indeed, may be construed as sexist). It also means acknowledging that tasks, such as children's librarianship and cataloging, are central to this field and as worthy of status and financial reward (if not more so) as computing expertise.

References

Abbott, Andrew. (1981). Status strain in the professions. *American Journal of Sociology, 86*(4), 819–835.

Allen, G.G. (1984). The proper status and functions of librarians in academic institutions. *The Australian Library Journal, 33*(4), 5–12.

American Library Association. (1981). *The ALA yearbook: A review of library events 1980* (Vol. 6). Chicago, IL: American Library Association.

_____. (1989). Constitution and bylaws. *ALA handbook of organization 1989/1990 and membership directory.* Chicago, IL: American Library Association.

_____. (1990). *ALA handbook of organization 1990/1991 and membership directory.* Chicago, IL: American Library Association.

Andreoli, Kathleen G.; Carollo, Jack R.; and Pottage, Marian W. (1988). Marketing strategies: Projecting an image of nursing that reflects achievement. *Nursing Administration Quarterly, 12*(4), 5–14.

Andrews, Janice. (1987). Social work public image building: "East side/West side" revisited. *The Social Service Review, 61*(3), 484–487.

Asheim, Lester. (1979). Librarians as professionals. *Library Trends, 27*(3), 225–257.

Ashley, Jo Ann. (1976). *Hospitals, paternalism, and the role of the nurse.* New York: Teachers College Press.

Association of Library and Information Science Education. (1990). *Directory issue, 1989–90.* Sarasota, FL.

Ballard, Thomas H. (1981). More books, not market surveys. *American Libraries, 12*(2), 76–78.

Barribeau, Susan. (1985). Resources for women: The Catalyst database. *Special Libraries, 76*(4), 290–294.

Baumgart, Alice J. (1980). Nurses and political action: The legacy of sexism. *Nursing Papers Perspective on Nursing, 12*(4), 6–15.

Bayless, Sandy. (1977). Librarianship is a discipline. *Library Journal, 102*(15), 1715–1717.

Bearman, Toni Carbo. (1987). The information society of the 1990s; blue sky and green pastures? *Online, 11*(1), 82–86.

Bell, Trudy E., and Janowski, Pat. (1988). The image benders. How the arts and media depict the engineer: Is the public deceived? *IEEE Spectrum, 25*(11), 132–136.

Bem, Sandra. (1983). The making of images: A psychological perspective. In Carolyn A. Williams (Ed.), *Image-Making in nursing* (pp. 39–45). American Academy of Nursing.

Benner. (1984). *From novice to expert: Excellence and power in clinical nursing practice.* Menlo Park, CA: Addison-Wesley.

Bennett, George E. (1988). *Librarians in search of science and identity: The elusive profession.* Metuchen, NJ: Scarecrow Press.

Bernard, Jessie (1981). *The female world.* New York: The Free Press.

———. (1983). The making of images: Theoretical perspective and implications for change—A sociological perspective. In Carolyn A. Williams (Ed.), *Image-making in nursing* (pp. 24–35). American Academy of Nursing.

Berry, John. (1985). New threats to the MLS? *Library Journal, 110*(5), 23–26.

———. (1986). The fundraising trap. *Library Journal, 111*(11), 4.

Biblarz, Dora; Capron, Margaret; Kennedy, Linda; Ross, Johanna; and Weinerth, David. (1975). Professional associations and unions: Future impact of today's decisions. *College & Research Libraries, 36*(2), 121–128.

Bille, Donald A. (1987). The nurse's image—a mirror of the self. *Today's OR Nurse, 9*(8), 7–8.

Birdsall, William F. (1980). Librarians and professionalism: Status measured by outmoded models. *Canadian Library Journal, 37,* 145–148.

Bishoff, Liz. (1989). Recruiting, what next? In Sheila S. Intner and Janet Swan Hill (Eds.), *Recruiting, educating and training cataloging librarians* (pp. 39–51). New York: Greenwood Press.

Blake, Fay M. (1983). Negative views. *Library Journal, 108,* 1345.

———. (1988). Information and poverty. In Jovian P. Lang (Ed.), *Unequal access to information resources: Problems and needs of the world's information poor* (pp. 9–12). Ann Arbor, MI: Pierian Press.

Blanke, Henry T. (1989). Librarianship and political values: neutrality or commitment? *Library Journal, 114*(12), 39–43.

Blum, Debra E. (1989). Professors of engineering continue to earn the highest average salaries. *The Chronicle of Higher Education, 35*(37), A14.

Blumenstein, Henry. (1988). Survival issues challenging family service agencies. *Social Casework: The Journal of Contemporary Social Work, 69*(2), 107–115.

Board's plan to hire CEO for Enoch Pratt draws fire. (1990). *American Libraries, 21*(4), 278.

Boissonnas, Christian. (1972). Heading in the right direction? ALA and professionalism. *American Libraries, 3*(9), 972–979.

Bourkoff, Vivienne R., and Wooldridge, Julia Binder. (1986). The image of libraries and librarians: Is it changing? *Public Library Quarterly, 6*(4), 55–63.

Brodie, Barbara. (1988). Voices in distant camps: The gap between nursing research and nursing practice. *Journal of Professional Nursing, 4*(5), 320–328.

Brown, Carol A. (1975). Women workers in the health service industry. *International Journal of Health Services, 5*(2), 173–184.

Buckland, Michael K. (1989). The roles of collections and the scope of collection development. *Journal of Documentation, 45*(3), 213–226.

Budget struck Stanford library merged with computer center. (1990). *American Libraries, 21*(9), 830.

Buschman, John. (1990). Asking the right questions about information technology. *American Libraries, 21*(11), 1026–1030.

Bush, Mary Ann, and Kjervik, Diane K. (1979). The nurse's self-image. *Nursing Times, 75*(17), 697–701.

Carey, John. (1979). Overdue: Taking issue with the issues. In Kathleen Weibel and Kathleen M. Heim (Eds.), *The role of women in librarianship 1876–1976: The entry, advancement, and struggle for equalization in one profession* (pp. 194–195). Phoenix, AZ: Oryx.

Carrigan, Zoe Henderson. (1978). Social workers in medical settings: who defines us? *Social Work in Health Care, 4*, 149–163.

Carter, Michael J., and Carter, Susan Boslego. (1981). Women's recent progress in the professions or, women get a ticket to ride after the gravy train has left the station. *Feminist Studies, 7*(3), 477–504.

Castledine, George. (1989). Opening the gates on gender traits. *Nursing Mirror, 156*(15), 16.

Caudle, Sharon L. and Levitan, Karen B. (1989). Improving the role of information resources management in federal information policies. In Charles R. McClure, Peter Hernon, and Harold C. Relyea (Eds.), *United States government information policy: Views and perspectives* (pp. 296–314). Norwood, NJ: Ablex.

Chafetz, Janet Saltzman. (1972). Women in social work. *Social Work, 17*(5), 12–18.

Chapman, Eunice. (1985). Once upon a time. *Nursing Mirror, 161*(7), 43.

Childers, Thomas. (1975). *The information-poor in America.* Metuchen, NJ: Scarecrow Press.

Cimbala, Diane J. (1987). The scholarly information center: An organizational model. *College & Research Libraries, 48*(5), 393–398.

Clearfield, Sidney M. (1977). Professional self-image of the social worker: Implications for social work education. *Journal of Education for Social Work, 13*, 23–30.

Coler, Marga Simon, and Sutherland, Michael. (1983). A semiquantitative method to assess role image in nursing through the application of semantics. *International Journal of Nursing Studies, 20*(4), 231–244.

Colson, John Calvin. (1980). Professional ideals and social realities: Some questions about the education of librarians. *Journal of Education for Librarianship, 21*(2), 91–108.

Commerton, Anne. (1975). Union or professional organization? A librarian's dilemma. *College & Research Libraries, 36*(2), 129–135.

Committee on Medical Education, The New York Academy of Medicine. (1977). Statement on nursing education: Status or service oriented? *Bulletin of the New York Academy of Medicine, 53*(5), 490–509.

Corley, Mary C., and Mauksch, Hans O. (1988). Registered nurses, gender and commitment. In Anne Statham, Eleanor M. Miller, and Hans O. Mauksch (Eds.), *The worth of women's work* (pp. 135–149). Albany, NY: State University of New York Press.

Covaleski, Mark A. (1981). The economic and professional legitimacy of nursing services. *Hospital & Health Services Administration, 26*(5), 75–91.

Crickman, Robin D. (1979). The emerging information professional. *Library Trends, 28*(2), 311–327.

Curran, Connie R., and Winder, Margo D. (1985). The cost of nursing's negative image. *Nursing Economics$, 3*(4), 252–253.

Curtin, Leah L. (1979). The nurse as advocate: A philosophical foundation for nursing. *Advances in Nursing Science, 1*(3), 1–10.

De Gennaro, Richard. (1989). Technology & access in an enterprise society. *Library Journal, 114*(16), 40–43.

DeWeese, L. Carroll. (1972). Status concerns and library professionalism. *College & Research Libraries, 33*(1), 31–38.

Dewey, Melvil. (1876). The library profession. *Library Journal, 1,* 5–6.

Dialog sues Chemical Abstracts, charging antitrust violations. (1990). *American Libraries, 21*(7), 623–625.

Divay, Gaby; Ducas, Ada M.; and Michaud-Oystryk, Nicole. (1987). Faculty perceptions of librarians at the University of Manitoba. *College & Research Libraries, 48*(1), 27–35.

Dolan, Andrew K. (1980). The legality of nursing associations serving as collective bargaining agents: The Arundel Case. *Journal of Health Politics, Policy and Law, 5*(1), 25–54.

Dowell, David R. (1977). Certification: More study needed. *Library Journal, 102*(15), 1720–1721.

Draper, Lewis. (1989). Who is going to look after the patients. *Canadian Medical Association Journal, 140,* 1217–1218.

Duxbury, Mitzi L. (1983). Discussion of Dr. Bernard's paper. In Carolyn A. Williams (ed.), *Image-Making in nursing* (pp. 36–38). American Academy of Nursing.

Dyer, Preston M. (1977). How professional is the BSW worker? *Social Work, 22(6),* 487–492.

Edwards, Adam. (1986). Exorcising the image. *Library Association Record, 88,* 399.

Edwards, Karlene K. (1989). Principals' perceptions of librarians: A survey. *School Library Journal, 35*(5), 28–31.

Edwards, Ralph M. (1975). The management of libraries and the professional functions of librarians. *Library Quarterly, 45*(2), 150–160.

Estabrook, Leigh. (1981a). Labor & librarians: The divisiveness of professionalism. *Library Journal, 106*(2), 125–127.

———. (1981b). Productivity, profit and libraries. *Library Journal, 106*(13), 1377–1380.

———. (1983). The human dimension of the catalog: Concepts and constraints in information seeking. *Library Resources & Technical Services, 27*(1), 68–75.

———. (1989). The growth of the profession. *College & Research Libraries, 50*(3), 287–296.

Euster, Gerald L. (1980). The occupational prestige of social work. *Journal of Sociology and Social Welfare, 7(2),* 273–284.

Evans, Dale; Fitzpatrick, Therese; and Howard-Ruben, Josie. (1983). A district takes action. *American Journal of Nursing, 83*(1), 52–54.

Fawcett, Jacqueline. (1984). The metaparadigm of nursing: Present status and future refinements. *Image: The Journal of Nursing Scholarship, 16*(3), 84–87.

Flanagan, Leo N. (1973). Professionalism dismissed. *College & Research Libraries*, *34*, 209–214.

Fortune, Anne E., and Hanks, Lou Loental. (1988). Gender inequities in early social work careers. *Social Work*, *33*(3), 221–226.

Freidson, Eliot. (1983). The theory of professions: State of the art. In Robert Dingwall and Philip Lewis (Eds.), *The sociology of the professions* (pp. 19–37). London: MacMillan.

Gallagher, Peter. (1987). Media image of nursing. *Nursing*, *3*(18), 674–676.

Galloway, Sue. (1985). Comparable worth adjustments: Yes. *American Libraries*, *16*(2), 92.

Garrison, Dee. (1979). *Apostles of culture: The public librarian and American society, 1876–1920*. New York: The Free Press.

Garson, Barbara. (1988). *The electronic sweatshop*. New York: Simon and Schuster.

Geismar, Ludwig L. (1984). Strengthening the scientific base of social work. In Miriam Dinerman and Ludwig L. Geismar (Eds.), *A quarter-century of social work education* (pp. 133–155). Baltimore, MD: National Association of Social Workers.

Glazer, Nathan. (1974). The schools of the minor professions. *Minerva*, *12*(3), 346–364.

Glazer, Penina Migdal, and Slater, Miriam. (1987). *Unequal colleagues: The entrance of women into the professions, 1890–1940*. New Brunswick, NJ: Rutgers University Press.

Goode, William J. (1961). The librarian: From occupation to profession? *Library Quarterly*, *31*, 306–320.

————. (1969). The theoretical limits of professionalization. In Amitai Etzioni (Ed.), *The semi-professions and their organization* (pp. 266–313). New York: Free Press.

Gorman, Michael. (1990). A bogus and dismal science or the eggplant that ate library schools. *American Libraries*, *21*(5), 462–463.

Govan, James F. (1988). The creeping invisible hand: Entrepreneurial librarianship. *Library Journal*, *113*(1), 35–38.

Gray, Carolyn M. (1987). Information technocracy: Prologue to a farce or a tragedy. *Information Technology and Libraries*, *6*(1), 3–9.

Gwinnup, Thomas. (1974). The failure of librarians to attain profession: The causes, the consequences, and the prospect. *Wilson Library Bulletin*, *48*, 482–490.

Haar, John M. (1986). The politics of information: Libraries & online retrieval systems. *Library Journal*, *111*(1), 40–43.

Hafter, Ruth. (1986). *Academic librarians and cataloging networks: Visibility, quality control, and professional status*. New York: Greenwood Press.

Hall, Marlene. (1984). Librarianship, a new type of profession. *The Australian Library Journal*, *33*(4), 23–29.

Hammer, Rita N., and Tufts, Margaret, A. (1985). Nursing's self-image—nursing education's responsibility. *Journal of Nursing Education*, *24*(7), 280–283.

Hammond, Merryl. (1990). Is nursing a semi-profession? *The Canadian Nurse*, *86*(2), 21–23.

Hanks, Gardner, and Schmidt, C. James. (1975). An alternative model of a profession for librarians. *College & Research Libraries*, *36*(3), 175–187.

Harris, Michael H. (1986). The dialectic of defeat: Antimonies in research in library and information science. *Library Trends, 34*(3), 515–531.

Harris, Roma. (1988). *Pay equity in predominantly female establishments: The library sector.* Toronto, Ontario: Report to the Minister of Labour by the Ontario Pay Equity Commission, Research Report I.

———; Michell, B. Gillian; and Cooley, Carol. (1985). The gender gap in library education. *Journal of Education for Library and Information Science, 25,* 167–176.

———; Monk, Susan; and Austin, Jill T. (1986). M.L.S. graduates survey: Sex differences in prestige and salary. *Canadian Library Journal, 43,* 149–153.

———, and Reid, K. Joanne. (1988). Career opportunities in library and information science: An analysis of Canadian job advertisements in the 1980s. *Canadian Journal of Information Science, 45,* 236–243.

———, and Sue-Chan, Christina. (1988). Cataloging and reference, circulation and shelving: Public library users and university students' perceptions of librarianship. *Library + Information Science Research, 10,* 95–107.

Harter, Stephen P., and Jackson, Susan M. (1988). Optical disc systems in libraries: Problems and issues. *RQ, 27*(4), 516–527.

Hash, Michael M. (1982). Nurses and health policy, *NLN Publications, 16,* 1–6.

Hayes, Robert M. (1988). Education and training of librarians. In *Rethinking the library in the information age* (vol. II, pp. 43–74). Washington DC: U.S. Department of Education.

———. (1989). The more things change. In Sheila S. Intner and Janet Swan Hill (Eds.), *Recruiting, educating and training cataloging librarians* (pp. 3–16). New York: Greenwood Press.

Heanue, Anne. (1988). Less access to less information by and about the United States Government. In Jovian P. Lang (Ed.), *Unequal access to information resources: Problems and needs of the world's information poor* (pp. 127–131). Ann Arbor, MI: Pierian Press.

Hearn, Jeff. (1982). Notes on patriarchy, professionalization and the semi-professions. *Sociology, 16*(2), 184–202.

Heim, Kathleen M. (1988). Librarians for the new millenium. In William E. Moen and Kathleen M. Heim (Eds.), *Librarians for the new millenium* (pp. 1–10). Chicago, IL: American Library Association.

Herbert, Jay. (1983). Down among the bedpans. *Nursing Times, 79*(26), 12–13.

Hernon, Peter. (1983). Keyes DeWitt Metcalf. In Wayne A. Wiegand (Ed.), *Leaders in American academic librarianship: 1925–1975* (pp. 213–235). Pittsburgh, PA: Beta Phi Mu.

———, and McClure, Charles R. (1987). *Federal information policies in the 1980s: Conflicts and issues.* Norwood, NJ: Ablex.

———, and McClure, Charles R. (1988). *Public access to government information: Issues, trends, and strategies* (2nd ed.). Norwood, NJ: Ablex.

———, and Pastine, Maureen. (1977). Student perceptions of academic librarians. *College & Research Libraries, 38*(2), 129–139.

Hildenbrand, Suzanne. (1985). Ambiguous authority and aborted ambition: Gender, professionalism, and the rise and fall of the welfare state. *Library Trends, 34*(2), 185–198.

———. (1989a). "Women's work" within librarianship: Time to expand the feminist agenda. *Library Journal, 114*(14), 153–155.

———. (1989b). The crisis in cataloging: A feminist hypothesis. In Sheila S. Intner and Janet Swan Hill (Eds.), *Recruiting, educating and training cataloging librarians* (pp. 207–225). New York: Greenwood Press.

Hinshaw, Ada Sue. (1983). The image of nursing research: Issues and strategies. *Western Journal of Nursing Research, 5*(3), 1–13.

Hole, Carol. (1990). The feminization of the public library. *American Libraries, 21*(11), 1076–1079.

Holley, Edward G. (1984). The Merwine case and the MLS: Where was the ALA? *American Libraries, 15*(5), 327–330.

Horn, Roger. (1975). The idea of academic library management. *College & Research Libraries, 36*(6), 464–472.

Horton, Forest Woody, Jr. (1982). The emerging information counselor. *Bulletin of the American Society for Information Science, 8*(5), 16–19.

How can I change the image of nursing? (1988). *NSNS/IMPRINT, 35*(4), 79–81.

How crucial librarianship is—who we are; what we do. (1990). *American Libraries, 21*(7), 689.

How the staff battled for chief's rights. (1977). *Library Association Record, 79*(4), 185–186.

Hughes, Helen MacGill; Hughes, Everett C.; and Deutscher, Irwin. (1958). *Twenty thousand nurses tell their story*. Philadelphia: Lippincott.

Humphreys, Nancy, and Dinerman, Miriam. (1984). Professionalizing social work. In Miriam Dinerman and Ludwig L. Geismar (Eds.), *A quarter-century of social work education* (pp. 181–214). Silver Spring, MD: National Association of Social Workers.

Image: How they're seeing us. (1986). *American Libraries, 17*(7), 502.

Inana, Marjorie. (1984). A review of selected reports on the status of American education with implications for home economics education. *Illinois Teacher of Home Economics, 27*(5), 170–174.

Interview. Toward a more profitable nursing image. (1984). *Nursing Success Today, 1*(4), 18–23.

Iversen, Roberta Rehner. (1987). Licensure: Help or hindrance to women social workers. *Social Casework, 68*(4), 229–233.

Janke, Richard V., and Nicholls, Paul T. (in press). University reference systems. *Journal of Academic Librarianship.*

Jansson, Bruce S., and Simmons, June. (1986). The survival of social work units in host organizations. *Social Work, 31*(5), 339–343.

Kadushin, Alfred. (1976). Men in a woman's profession. *Social Work, 21*(6), 440–447.

Kalisch, Beatrice J., and Kalisch, Philip A. (1976). A discourse on the politics of nursing. *Journal of Nursing Administration, 6*(3), 29–34.

———. (1983a). Anatomy of the image of the nurse: Dissonant and ideal models. In Carolyn A. Williams (Ed.), *Image-making in nursing* (pp. 3–23). American Academy of Nursing.

———. (1983b). Improving the image of nursing. *American Journal of Nursing, 83*(1), 48–52.

_____. (1984). The Dionne quintuplets legacy: Establishing the "Good doctor and his loyal nurse" image in American culture. *Nursing & Health Care, 5*(5), 242–251.

Kalisch, Philip A., and Kalisch, Beatrice J. (1989). Perspectives on improving nursing's public image. *Nursing & Health Care, 1*(1), 10–15.

_____. (1981). The image of psychiatric nurses in motion pictures. *Perspectives in Psychiatric Care, 24*(3/4), 116–129.

_____. (1986). A comparative analysis of nurse and physician characters in the entertainment media. *Journal of Advanced Nursing, 11*(2), 179–195.

Karger, H. Jacob. (1983). Science, research, and social work: Who controls the profession? *Social Work, 28*(3), 200–205.

Katz, Bill. (1983). The uncertain realities of reference service. *Library Trends, 31*(3), 363–374.

Katz, Fred. (1969). Nurses. In Amitai Etzioni (Ed.), *The semi-professions and their organization* (pp. 54–81). New York: Free Press.

Katz, Raul Luciano. (1988). *The information society.* New York: Praeger.

Keddy, Barbara; Gillis, Margaret Jones; Jacobs, Pat; Burton, Heather; and Rogers, Maureen. (1986). The doctor-nurse relationship: An historical perspective. *Journal of Advanced Nursing, 11,* 745–753.

Kelly, Lucie S. (1989). Updating nursing's image. *Nursing Outlook, 37*(1), 17.

Kniffel, Leonard. (1989). New York greets Jesuit director of NYPL with praise, qualms. *American Libraries, 20*(4), 279.

_____. (1990). What's so bad about a shortage? *American Libraries, 21*(6), 476.

Koenig, Michael E.D. (1990). Buttering the toast evenly. Library school closings at Columbia and Chicago are tragic; but they don't have to signal a trend. *American Libraries, 21*(8), 723–726.

Kooker, Barbara Molina. (1986). The corporate image of a nurse executive. *Nursing Management, 17*(2), 52–55.

Kraft, Joan Federico. (1987). *Women, computers and information work.* Unpublished Ph.D. dissertation, The American University.

Krislov, Alex. (1981). Engineering certification: Enhanced status or stolen titles? *Power Transm Des, 23,* 50–53.

Larson, Elaine. (1984). The current status of nursing research. *Nursing Forum, 21*(3), 131–134.

Larson, Magali Sarfatti. (1977). *The rise of professionalism.* Berkeley: University of California Press.

Lause, Timothy. (1979). Status enhancement and social problem concerns: An essay on the course of state social work associations. *Journal of Sociology and Social Welfare, 6*(4), 546–554.

Lerner, Harriet Goldhor. (1990). Problems for profit? *The Women's Review of Books, 7*(7), 15–16.

Lester, June. (1990). Education for librarianship: A report card. *American Libraries, 21*(6), 580–586.

Lewin, Ellen. (1977). Feminist ideology and the meaning of work: The case of nursing. *Catalyst, 10/11,* 78–103.

Lewis, Dennis A. (1980). Today's challenge—tomorrow's choice: Change or be changed or the doomsday scenario Mk2. *Journal of Information Science, 2*(2), 59–74.

Licensing librarians: What Indiana gives, it can also take away. (1990). *American Libraries, 21*(4), 285–286.

Lidgate, D. (1988). The engineer in society. *IEE Proceedings, 135,* 247–252.

Lindberg, Carolyn H. (1990). Certification, status, and salaries. *Journal of Education for Library and Information Science, 31*(2), 157–161.

Lippman, Doris T., and Ponton, Karen S. (1989). Nursing's image on the university campus. *Nursing Outlook, 37*(1), 24–27.

Lowe, Gary R. (1985). The graduate only debate in social work education, 1931–1959, and its consequences for the profession. *Journal of Social Work Education, 21*(3), 52–62.

Lundberg, Norma J. (1991). *The social organization of birth control information in public libraries.* Unpublished doctoral dissertation, University of Western Ontario.

MacCleave-Frazier, Anne, and Murray, Elouise Comeau. (1984). A framework for reconceptualizing home economics. *Canadian Home Economics Journal,* pp. 69–73.

Markuson, Barbara Evans. (1976). Bibliographic systems, 1945–1976. *Library Trends, 25*(1), 311–328.

Marshall, Judi. (1989). Re-visioning career concepts: A feminist invitation. In Michael B. Arthur, Douglas T. Hall, and Barbara S. Lawrence (Eds.), *Handbook of career theory* (pp. 275–291). Cambridge: Cambridge University Press.

Mauksch, Hans O., and Campbell, James D. (1985). Political imperatives for nursing in a stereotyping world. *NLN Publications, 41-1985,* 222–229.

McClure, Charles R.; Bishop, Ann; and Doty, Philip. (1989). Federal information policy development: The role of the Office of Management and Budget. In Charles R. McClure, Peter Hernon, and Harold C. Relyea (Eds.), *United States government information policy: Views and perspectives.* Norwood, NJ: Ablex.

McDermott, Judy C. (1984). The professional status of librarians: A realistic and unpopular analysis. *Journal of Library Administration, 5*(3), 17–21.

McReynolds, Rosalee (1985a). A heritage dismissed. *Library Journal, 110*(18), 25–31.

——— . (1985b). Negative 'image.' *American Libraries, 16,* 213.

Meade, Cathy D. (1986). Control the media with power. *Nursing Success Today, 3*(12), 24–27.

Meltz, Noah M. (1988). *The shortage of registered nurses: An analysis in a labour market context.* Toronto, Ontario: The Registered Nurses Association of Ontario.

Meyer, Richard W. (1980). Library professionalism and the democratic way. *The Journal of Academic Librarianship, 6*(5), 277–281.

——— . (1981). Faculty status and academic librarians: Are there second thoughts? *North Carolina Libraries, 39,* 41–47.

Meyers, Shirley. (1988). Certification of home economists: A program of the American Home Economics Association. *Canadian Home Economics Journal, 38*(1), 20–21.

Miller, Barbara K. (1988). A model for professionalism in nursing. *Today's OR Nurse, 10*(9), 18–23.

Morrisey, Locke J., and Case, Donald O. (1988). There goes my image: The perceptions of male librarians by colleague, student, and self. *College & Research Libraries, 49*(5), 453–464.

Mudge, Charlotte R. (1984). *Bargaining unit composition and negotiation outcomes: A study of academic and public library personnel in Ontario.* Unpublished doctoral dissertation, University of Toronto.

_____. (1986). Mixed unit bargaining: are librarians losing? *Canadian Library Journal, 43*(3), 193–194.

Muff, Janet. (1988). Meeting the goddesses: Exploring the positive feminine in nursing stereotypes. *National Student Nurses Association Imprint, 35*(4), 43–49.

Murphy, Ellen K. (1987). The professional status of nursing: A view from the courts. *Nursing Outlook, 35*(1), 12–15.

Myers, Shirley. (1988). Certification of home economists: A program of the American Home Economics Association. *Canadian Home Economics Journal, 38*(1), 20–21.

National Librarians Association: Constitution. (1989). *National Librarian, 14*(1), 4–5.

National Library of Canada. (1990). Response to the recommendation of The Task Force on Classification and Occupational Group Structures regarding the Library Science group. Ottawa, Ontario.

Neal, James G. (1989). The evolving public/technical services relationship: New opportunities for staffing the cataloging function. In Sheila S. Intner and Janet Swan Hill (Eds.), *Recruiting, educating and training cataloging librarians* (pp. 111–119). New York: Greenwood Press.

Nelson, Bonnie R. (1980). The chimera of professionalism. *Library Journal, 105*(17), 2029–2033.

Nelson, Milo G. (1987). Pell mell back to square one. *Wilson Library Bulletin, 62*(2), 4.

Nerad, Maresi. (1988). *The vicious cycle of gender and status at the University of California at Berkeley, 1918–1954.* Paper presented at the Annual Meeting of the Association for the study of Higher Education, St. Louis, MO.

Newmeyer, Jody. (1976). The image problem of the librarian: femininity and social control. *Journal of Library History, 11*, 44–67.

Nielsen, Brian. (1980). Online bibliographic searching and the deprofessionalization of librarianship. *Online Review, 4*(3), 215–224.

North, John. (1977). Librarianship: A profession? *Canadian Library Journal, 34*, 253–257.

O'Leary, Mick. (1987). The information broker: A modern profile. *Online, 11*(6), 24–30.

O'Neill, June. (1985). Comparable worth adjustments: No. *American Libraries, 16*(2), 93–94.

O'Reilly, Robert C., and O'Reilly, Marjorie I. (1981). *Librarians and labor relations.* Westport, CT: Greenwood Press.

Para, A. (1989). Thanks for the invitation. *Colorado Libraries, 15*(1), 12–13.

Paris, Marion. (1990). Why library schools fail. *Library Journal, 115*(16), 38–42.

Parson, Willie L. (1984). User perspective on a new paradigm for librarianship. *College & Research Libraries, 45*(5), 370–373.

Partridge, Kay B. (1978). Nursing values in a changing society. *Nursing Outlook,* *26,* 356–360.

Plaiss, Mark. (1990). Libraryland: Pseudo-intellectuals and semi-dullards. *American Libraries, 21,* 588–589.

Porter, Rosemary T.; Porter, Michael J.; and Lower, Mary S. (1989). Enhancing the image of nursing. *Journal of Nursing Administration, 19*(2), 36–40.

Power of images. (1988). *Journal of Academic Librarianship, 14*(3), 139.

Rasmussen, Cathy. (1988). What's your I.Q.? *The Sourdough, 25*(2), 12.

Rayner, Claire. (1984). What do the public think of nurses? *Nursing Times, 80*(35), 28–31.

Reeves, Dianne M.; Underly, Nancy K.; and Goddard, Nannette L. (1983). How to improve your image. *Nursing Life, 3*(3), 57–58.

Reeves, William Joseph. (1980). *Librarians as professionals.* Lexington, MA: Lexington Books.

Richards, Diane, and Elliot, Paula. (1988). How others see us. *College & Research Libraries News, 49*(7), 422–425.

Rinneard, Beverley. (1975). Nurses' professional image and collective bargaining. *Hospital Administration in Canada, 17*(6), 64.

Robbins-Carter, Jane B.; Sherrer, Johannah; Jakubs, Deborah; and Lowry, Charles B. (1985). Reactions to "1985 to 1995: The next decade in academic librarianship," Parts I and II. *College & Research Libraries, 46*(4), 309–319.

Robinson, Barbara M. (1983). Librarianship under attack. *Library Journal, 108*(3), 347–348.

Rossi, Peter H. (1961). Discussion. *Library Quarterly, 31*(4), 380–381.

Rowe, Richard R. (1987). You, the CIO. Can librarians make the jump to "Chief Information Officer"? *American Libraries, 18*(4), 297.

Sadler, Catharine. (1984). Firm-jawed or dewy-eyed? *Nursing Mirror, 159*(20), 43.

Salvage, Jane. (1983). Changing the image. *International Nursing Review, 30*(6) 181–182.

San Diego PL faces layoffs, possible 62% budget cut. (1990). *American Libraries, 21*(5), 398.

Santo, Brian. (1988). From the mirror. A just-concluded poll reveals some unexpected self-perceptions. *IEEE Spectrum, 25*(11), 136–138.

Sapp, Gregg. (1987). What the librarian didn't see in the mirror: Aspects of the professional stereotype. *Catholic Library World, 58*(3), 135–136.

Schiller, Anita R. (1974). Women in librarianship. In Melvin J. Voight (Ed.), *Advances in librarianship* (Vol. 4, pp. 103–147). New York: Academic Press.

———. (1981). Shifting boundaries in information. *Library Journal, 106*(7), 705–709.

Schlachter, Gail. (1973). Quasi unions and organizational hegemony within the library field. *Library Quarterly, 43*(3), 185–198.

———. (1976). Professionalism v. unionism. *Library Trends, 25*(2), 451–473.

Schuman, Patricia Glass. (1982). Information justice. *Library Journal, 107,* 1060–1066.

Scott, W. Richard. (1969). Professional employees in a bureaucratic structure: Social work. In Amitai Etzioni (Ed.), *The semi-professions and their organization* (pp. 82–140). New York: Free Press.

Shapiro, Fred R. (1984). The name of our profession. *Legal Reference Services*

Quarterly, 4(2), 117–120.

Shera, Jesse H. (1976). Failure and success: Assessing a century. *Library Journal, 101*(1), 281–287.

Silver, Linda R. (1988). Deference to authority in the feminized professions. *School Library Journal, 34,* 21–27.

Simpson, Richard L., and Simpson, Ida Harper. (1969). Women and bureaucracy in the semi-professions. In Amitai Etzioni (Ed.), *The semi-professions and their organization* (pp. 196–265). New York: Free Press.

Siporin, Max. (1984). A future for social work education. In Miriam Dinerman and Ludwig L. Geismar (Eds.), *A quarter-century of social work education* (pp. 237–251). Baltimore, MD: National Association of Social Workers.

Slater, Margaret. (1987). Careers and the occupational image. *Journal of Information Science, 13*(6), 335–342.

Smith, Barbara. (1989). A strategic approach to online user fees in public libraries. *Library Journal, 114*(2), 33–36.

Specht, Harry. (1972). The deprofessionalization of social work. *Social Work, 17*(2), 3–15.

Stephany, Theresa M. (1985). We need just one door to nursing. *RN, 48,* 64–65.

Stephens, Elsie. (1986). Professional status of librarianship revisited. *Journal of Library Administration, 7*(1), 7–12.

Stevens, Norman. (1988). Our image in the 1980s. *Library Trends, 36*(4), 825–851.

Stokes, Roy. (1967). The trading stamp mentality. *Library Journal, 92*(18), 3595–3600.

Strasen, Leann. (1989). Self concept: Improving the image of nursing. *Journal of Nursing Administration, 19*(1), 4–5.

Taylor, David C. (1989). References ROMs: Six implications for libraries building CD-ROM database services. *American Libraries, 20*(5), 452–454.

Thomas, Carol. (1990). Nurses benefit from feminism: Fenwick. *Hospital Nurse, 3*(9), 14.

Tifft, Susan. (1990, January 15). Get me a ladder at the library. *Time,* pp. 54–55.

Todd, Katherine. (1985). Collective bargaining and professional associations in the library field. *Library Quarterly, 55*(3), 284–299.

Toren, Nina. (1975). Deprofessionalization and its sources. *Sociology of Work and Occupations, 2*(4), 323–337.

University of Toronto. (1989). *Faculty of library and information science calendar, 1989–1990.* Toronto, Ontario.

Vagianos, Louis. (1973). The librarian and the garbageman. Professionalism reconsidered. *Library Journal, 98*(3), 391–393.

————, and Lesser, Barry. (1988). Information policy issues: Putting library policy in context. In *Rethinking the library in the information age* (Vol. II, pp. 9–41). Washington, DC: U.S. Department of Education.

Veaner, Allen B. (1985). 1985 to 1995: The next decade in academic librarianship, Part I. *College & Research Libraries, 46*(3), 209–229; Part II, *46*(4), 309–319.

Vice, Katherine. (1988). Professional status—not the be all or end all. *Canadian Library Journal, 45,* 23–27.

Vincenti, Virginia B. (1982). Toward a clearer professional identity. *Journal of Home Economics, 74,* 20–25.

Wallace, Linda. (1989). The image—and what you can do about it in the Year of the Librarian. *American Libraries, 20*(1), 22–25.

Warner, Sandra L.; Ross, M. Candice; and Clark, Lori. (1988). An analysis of entry into practice arguments. *Image: Journal of Nursing Scholarship, 20*(4), 212–216.

Webster, Denise. (1985). Medical students' views of the role of the nurse. *Nursing Research, 34*(5), 313–317.

Webster, Frank, and Robins, Kevin. (1986). *Information technology: A Luddite analysis.* Norwood, NJ: Ablex.

Weibel, Kathleen. (1976). Toward a feminist profession. *Library Journal, 101*(1), 263–267.

Weiss, Sandra J. (1983). Role differentiation between nurse and physician: Implications for nursing. *Nursing Research, 32*(3), 133–139.

Welch, Martha J. (1980). Dysfunctional parenting of a profession. *Nursing Outlook, 28*(12), 724–727.

Werrell, Emily, and Sullivan, Laura. (1987). Faculty status for academic librarians: A review of the literature. *College & Research Libraries, 48*(2), 95–103.

Wessel, Andrew E. (1976). *The social use of information—ownership and access.* New York: Wiley.

Whatley, Alice Elrod. (1974). Indignation, an impetus for change. *Illinois Teacher of Home Economics, 18*(1), 10–13.

White, Herbert S. (1986). Respect for librarians & librarian self respect. *Library Journal, 111*(2), 58–59.

———. (1990). Pseudo-libraries and semi-teachers, Parts I and II. *American Libraries,* Part I, *21*(2), 103–106; Part II, *21*(3), 262–266.

Whittaker, Martha. (1988). Network net worth: A cataloger's view. *Technicalities, 8*(1), 12–13.

Wikler, Marvin E. (1980). Saving face in the status race. *Health and Social Work, 5*(2), 27–33.

Wilson, Pauline. (1981). Professionalism under attack! *Journal of Academic Librarianship, 7*(5), 283–290.

———. (1982). *Stereotype and status: Librarians in the United States.* Westport, CT: Greenwood Press.

———. (1984). ALA, the MLS, and professional employment: An observer's field guide to the issues. *American Libraries, 15,* 563–566.

Winter, Michael F. (1988). *The culture and control of expertise.* New York: Greenwood Press.

Yelaja, Shankar A. (1985). *An introduction to social work practice in Canada.* Scarborough, Ontario: Prentice-Hall.

Zwiep, Donald N. (1980). A question of credibility. *Mechanical Engineering, 102,* 29–31.

Author Index

Subject Index